Unfortunate Incidents

1996-2000

Anthony Gancarski

DIVERSITY, INC.
Madison, WI

THIS IS A CREATIVE WORK. ALL OF THE PEOPLE AND PLACES CONTAINED HEREIN ARE IMAGINARY, ANY RESEMBLANCE TO PERSONS OR PLACES LIVING OR DEAD IS PURELY COINCIDENTAL.

FIRST PRINTING JANUARY 2001

ISBN–0-9704098-3-4

MANUFACTURED IN THE UNITED STATES
(MILWAUKEE, WI TO BE SPECIFIC)

PUBLISHED BY DIVERSITY INC.
P.O. BOX 8573
MADISON, WI 53708

COVER PHOTO BY
BENJAMIN M. LEROY

To Allison,

who was my muse for
the longest time

Contents

Short Stories:

Poems:

Unfortunate Incidents:
Poems and Short Stories, 1996-2000

(1) 10 Year Reunion

I've come to know entire episodes of Kojak by heart, right down to being able to hum the appropriate incidental music between swatches of dialogue. I've become so obsessed with Dragnet and Rockford that I toyed with the idea of learning HTML to assemble fan sites, just before a freak power surge rendered my computer and its peripherals beyond use. Entire days have been spent in thrall to the utter sprawl of digital cable; its vicissitudes, its ebbs and flows, its yearnings and burnings, melodramatic plots, characters two-dimensional only on very special episodes, and I haven't regretted nearly enough of it.

I'm what you might call marginally employed. Of course, to put that down as an occupation if one went on a game show or whatever wouldn't fly. Far better to label one's self a freelance writer. A Freelance Artist. A Freelance whatever.

Truth is, though, I didn't freelance at much of anything. I'd eschewed the diurnal lifestyle, opting instead to lapse into slumber around five AM when my mother's coffee would begin its pre-ordained percolations. At all times, I'd make sure to wake up before my mother got home from work, always being careful to leave a folded, wrinkled copy of the classifieds on one of the house's more public surfaces – the kitchen table, the bathroom counter – ballasted by its complementary prop: a blue ballpoint pen, which simultaneously moored it to the surface while providing evidence that I was looking for a job, that I was a good son.

Just a little off-track, was all. Like my mother always said, things will look up.

It was a typically oppressive late-August Friday afternoon in Jacksonville, Florida. I examined the postcard in my hand, that had been in my wallet, that had been on my dresser, that had seldom been cleaved from my consciousness since it had arrived in the mail three weeks prior. The front of it was all shimmer and grace; a glossy picture of toothy-smiled, attractive couples slowdancing. Two couples. The contact was affectionate, intimate even, yet at the same time chaste. People secure enough in their love for each other not to flash it on the dance floor like some sort of gaudy counterfeit jewel; they could hold each other and not seemingly begrudge the world while doing so. I admired this.

The back of the card was text, arranged tastefully in a deep red, a traffic-light green, and basic black. I very well could have committed the text to memory even after having read it a handful of times, but I in fact had read the card every time I gave it a thought. "ReunionMakers invites you to your 10th Bonneavue High School Reunion, to be held August 26 at the Dorchester Hotel, Jacksonville!" The card went on to encourage me to dress semi-formally, and to be sure to register in advance for this gala affair so as to be guaranteed food and reduced price admission. It was too late to register in advance, though; the reunion was that night, just hours away.

The card evoked any number of memories. I thought of the bonfire I built in my mother's yard after getting home from the graduation ceremony, and remembered how quickly my gasoline-soaked high school effects – virgin yearbooks, unmolested by the sloppy penmanship of my Bonneavue classmates; report cards; essays; cap, gown, and tassel – went up in flame. The smoke billowed blackly for a matter of instants against the bloodletting sunset, and the smell of plastic overcame the toxins of the pine trees that so dominated the parcel behind my mother's house.

10 Year Reunion

The girls who'd rejected me: the bottle-blonde Riviera twins, not much to look at but with reputations as convoluted as the ingredient labels on Hostess cakes; Ashley Witter, the class president, who always had a ready smile (until I called her house one too many times, and her boyfriend, seconded by the front court of the basketball team, showed me that you didn't need a restraining order to get a guy to leave a girl alone); and so many others. How many times had skirts averted their glances from me? The fake phone numbers, the lowered voices, the notes slipped into my locker, the abasement of my family's cars and house alike.

And to think, I was to sport semi-formal attire. Never had I an occasion to even find out what that was.

For a period of time, I sat on the couch. My legs were parted slightly, my jaw slackened at a rakish angle. I held the card cupped loosely in my hands, as if being careful not to break its birdlike frame. I was distracted from my aggregate of DSM-IV behaviors by the grating digitality of the phone. I picked up as I looked at the Caller ID.

"Hi, Mom." I considered the card once more, then put it on the sofa beside me.

"You sound like crap. What's wrong?" Behind her I could hear dry cleaning equipment going through dry cleaning paces; she was at work, at the Your Friendly Cleaners she owned.

"Nothing. Just thinking." Thinking, thinking, thinking; I imagined myself in an old-school anti-drug video, the gerund echoing as I was sucked into a vacuum of barbiturates and filtered sitar music.

"About what?" She cleared her throat, then asked me if I wanted to come have lunch with her. "I can take a break whenever."

It was like having a girlfriend, without the problem of sex, but with those messy Oedipal hangups. I thought of Howard Sprague on the Andy Griffith show, and felt bilious panic fomenting in my throat.

"Er, no. I've got – plans."

A pause in conversation; for a few beats I focused on the treadmill pitter-pat coming from the receiver.

10 YEAR REUNION

"Honey, I've got to go. But don't worry too much about looking for a job today. Why don't you go see a movie, or hang out with that girl Mindy? You like her, don't you?"

Mindy: a tangle of unhappy laments. Done wrong by various boyfriends, parents, employers, and so forth. 19 to my 28. She was great until I got to know her. Then the weight gain hit, brought on by her unfortunate addiction to Chinese takeout. When her hips and thighs turned to soggy mounds, I started noticing the waft of dead cigarettes in her wake. The fine layer of grime on her outfits. I started to realize that, as opposed to girls about whom people used to say *you don't know where they've been*, I did know where Mindy had been, and had no plans to visit myself.

I bid my mother farewell, and let her know with a sharp exhale of exasperation that Mindy was not an option.

Without even bothering to check what Gunsmoke was on, I cleared out of my mother's house, and subsequently peeled out the driveway with all of the violent authority of a teenager taking liberties with himself. I couldn't even think at my mother's; she was too well-meaning, and I was too entrenched in my failings, which stretched out like the Begats in the Bible. What the hell was wrong with me? I couldn't even call up this dingbat teenager to solve the problem of sex! And to top it off, I couldn't decide if I wanted to go to a reunion of people who spent four years making mock of me. Four years of cockteases and gym class humiliations, and I wanted an epilogue?

I drove toward the mall, then turned around with about a half-mile to go, before the line of SUV's settled into an impassive crawl. Money wasn't the issue; my mother had always taken care to give me copies of all of her department store credit cards. I could've had my pick of any overpriced outfit in any store, really. I could've just asked my mother what semi-formal meant – she had to know, she was a dry cleaner – or I could've just borrowed a suitable outfit from the formidable rack of clothes that had yet to be picked up. But I couldn't deal with the mall; it was too sterile, and I was too conscious of myself. My myriad odors: morning breath in mid-afternoon; the scent of roast chicken that seemed to rise from my torso; the delicate flakiness of my scalp, my hair unwashed for days.

The mall was no place for me, with its perfectly formed teenage bodies (I thought of a song I wrote and played at a local open-mike to some acclaim; "She Said She Was 18"), with its ruthless mélange of well-dressed, unctuous folks who barely waited until your back was turned to stick the knife in. There was no way. So, with my car headed safely in the opposite direction, I pushed the air conditioner to its limits and let myself bathe in the rancorous, yet oddly relaxing, tones of Sports Talk Radio.

I never had been much of an athlete in school, as if you couldn't glean that from the above descriptions. And after high school passed and I faded into collegiate mediocrity and obscurity, I still wasn't much for sports. But when I settled into my life's current "groove" and came to understand that this life was what I had and what I would have until something outside me imposed its will on me, I grew to accept the mantle handed down to me by generations of distended manhood that had preceded me: sports fan.

Go Jaguars! Run through your 11-5 seasons, find a way to talk of the so-called character on your Jesus Freak football club until collapsing like pacemaker patients in a room full of microwave ovens. Go Gators! Accept the deification of so-called star athletes; graceful supplicancy means that perhaps someone somewhere will toss some scraps to the screaming throngs of Beta males and below in the cheap seats. Tricks with nice racks but Nixonian faces? Sure, that would be fine, sir; here's your change!

It was all very easy, really, to accept the pre-ordained escape valves provided by my society. In that spirit of community, I cheerfully turned on the radio, nodding my head contentedly as I listened to a stuttering fool from Dubuque getting "run" because "his take sucked." And when a subsequent caller drew a mental picture of exactly what he'd like to do to Monday Night Football sideline fleshpot Melissa Stark, I grooved on that too, mentally running my tongue along the appropriately curved outline of her breast, as her eyes Xed out and her little porcine nose turned upwards. Yes.

10 Year Reunion

Eventually, all of that came to an end. I had made the final turn into my buddy Chad's apartment complex, Okefenokee Acres, which thirty years ago might well have been a tasteful assemblage of buildings, nestled snugly amongst each other, sheltered from the clogged thoroughfare at its rim that promised "country living in a city location" or some such swill and garbage by a mixture of majestic old-growth trees and tender, yet potential-laden, saplings. As it was though, Okefenokee Acres was a slum. A patchwork quilt of buildings yellowing like smokers' teeth, all in dire need of pressure washing if not petroleum-aided immolation, with unhappy late-model cars parked willy-nilly on the concrete in front of them as if abandoned by some squalling toddler.

I was sure to lock my car doors and check them twice as if some malevolent force had unlocked them from within when I wasn't paying attention.

I knocked on Chad's door with no particular sense of expectation. I hadn't been invited over, but it didn't matter; our lives were mirrored images of sleep after sunrise and garden-variety sloth, though his was excused by a penchant for spirits, weed, and such. I was just a social drinker, and I saw drugs as pointless, so I didn't even have that excuse for not living up to my vaunted Gifted class potential.

He opened the door, his hair surprisingly combed, his face freshly shaved. From his living room I could hear the nausea-inducing effervescence of daytime children's television. "The kid's over," I said by way of greeting, jabbing my index finger in the direction of that sound that might as well have been my own evisceration.

"Yeah," he said through a mouth full of teeth. Chad always hoped against hope, which was admirable, one supposed, but entirely moronic when one considered the facts of his life. He lived off disability, and spent the bulk of his time writing love poems for a woman who routinely rubbed him out with less ceremony or surprise than she would a stain on a white shirt. A woman engaged to an entertainment lawyer, in Los Angeles.

"It's Staci's last weekend here. They're moving out west next week, so it's my last day with her." He looked down at his feet for a second, then managed to look me straight in the eye again; I couldn't imagine how. "You're welcome to chill with us this afternoon if you want. But let's get out of here to do it."

For a fleeting moment as he retrieved his kid from the living room and blundered through his house looking for his wallet and keys, I was filled with something close to love. I didn't know how he'd get through the upcoming months, and knowing me, I'd keep my distance through the worst of it. But I knew that Chad was no freelancer of the heart, not in the way I was.

"I'll drive," I proposed to my default friend and his sullen daughter, who had already put on earphones and raised the volume to levels that obliterated external interference. Chad grinned at me sheepishly, and I thought about patting him on the back. There was no way to do that without an awkward movement on at least one of our parts, however, so I unlocked the car doors with an economy of both motion and time. "Hot as hell out here," I said, my voice cracking for a reason I couldn't name.

Our sarcophagus on wheels rolled through the rush hour traffic, as we looked for a destination within both the city limits and the realm of plausibility. My suggestions had been shot down by Chad, who kept looking back at his little girl, cocooned safely from us by whatever mass-produced dreck for children she was listening to. Then, suddenly, he called for me to make a sharp right into a strip mall. Then a sharp left; I felt I was driving with an Etch-a-Sketch. "Park wherever, dude."

We found a spot right in front of the building, somewhat surprising since it was late and getting later on a Friday afternoon. "Flamingo Bar and Grill", I read off the awning.

"Yeah, Staci's hungry, poor girl." I cocked my eyebrow at Chad, not quite swallowing his line of bull. "You been here? It's a nice place. Good people." I got out of the car and stared forward as I made my way toward the glass doors.

Happy Hour at the Flamingo wasn't too damned happy, if you asked me. Mausoleum lighting showcased men in their so-called golden years spread out here and there at the bar, nursing mugs of beer. Over the right hand corner of the back wall a television's cathode rays burned wanly, and I figured the people had better be damned good, as the description "nice place" didn't quite cut it.

"It's early," Chad said, as his daughter had made her way to a pinball machine by the restrooms.

"Yeah, I'll bet this place really picks up later on," I answered acidly.

We got two stools and two watery domestic beers, and trained our eyes toward the television. Chad gestured toward the set. "Damned shame. Those kids were in the prime of their lives, and those bastards cut them down."

Recycled images flickered both on the 19-inch monitor and in my mind. I remembered all the post Columbine hype, as we genuflected yet again before the altar of blonde hair, blue eyed, acceptably-coiffed, toned and tanned role models and cried crocodile tears when they met with unexpected tragedy. "Horseshit, Chad."

He looked at me as if I'd casually mentioned knowing his wife in the Biblical sense. "Do what?"

"Horseshit. It doesn't matter what happened there, to them, or whatever. You think you know so much about Columbine, because some dipshit news organization pumps your head full of facts? Come on. Don't be a moron. You have no clue what those kids were going through, but you know some bad shit happened to them to pull a kamikaze act on their high school."

Chad shot me the *I think you'd better leave* look, but then realized that we were at a bar and that I'd driven. It occurred to me that Chad didn't know what might have driven people to plan a high school holocaust, and that he probably didn't want to know. Though in all honesty I could've lived without the knowledge myself.

I stared at the television for a bit as it cycled through local ad spots, then felt a bristling against my leg; Chad's daughter, calling out. "Daddy, I'm hungry." Her eyes glistened soulfully and, as if in a pose of concession, her headphones were wrapped around her neck.

Chad was deep into a second beer already, and showed no indication of slowing down. "Hey, Ivan," he called to the bartender. "You got something to eat back there?"

The girl looked at me doubtfully, and I returned her gaze stoically. Ivan ducked behind a leather door and then reemerged about a minute later with what looked like a block of ice. "Frozen hamburgers." Things didn't bode too well for Staci's last evening with Dad.

I stood up. "Hey, I'll run and get her a Happy Meal."

Chad's face brightened. "Happy Meal! Hey, Stace, what do you say? You want to go on a run with your uncle."

She shook her head slowly, yet emphatically. I was to ride alone. That was fine.

Nothing but commercials on the radio. Nothing but a line at the McDonald's, a line so prohibitively long that it took very little thought for me not to even think of braving it. I found myself driving north, found the traffic surprisingly abated. There was no rush to get back to the Flamingo, not really.

I felt under my seat, and the reassuring cool, utilitarian steel was still there, as if stowed away for a moment like this. The Dorchester was just ten minutes away. Maybe fifteen if I hit some lights, but still plenty of time to be there early, to see everyone as they filed in. Things would look up. Things were looking up.

(2) Bachelor Father

I looked her over – gap teeth, split ends, Polynesian extraction and all – running the false promise of the Adult Services classified ad through my mind. "When I'm good I'm good, but when I'm bad I'm better." The ad claimed the requisite 36/24/36, but Brittany – the alleged college Junior in front of me in a baggy black Victoria's Secret negligée – didn't really have any hourglass shape. Just as I was, she was more or less shaped like a potato, lumps and all.

I had my wallet out at this point and was fingering a thin stack of ATM-fresh twenties nervously. Two hundred my ass. Maybe thirty in a pinch, a dark room in a strobelit club after three or four beers. The best I could come up with was "I thought you were supposed to be blonde. W-weren't you the b-blond one in the ad?" I was stuttering, right there in front of a half-naked erotic masseuse who smelled cold and greasy, vaguely like bowling alley French fries. Two hundred was two hundred, and was much farther than I was willing to go for Brittany.

She smiled at me, sat down on the bed, and patted the comforter in a last-ditch effort to get me to relax. But her gestures sagged from a lack of conviction. I just stood there and took it all in – the K-Mart looking bed with its flimsy canopy; the dog-eared, glossy B&D magazines on the floor. A stereo in the corner playing one of those Favorites of The 70s, 80s, and 90s stations (I knew what it was even though it was on commercial, a pleasant-sounding white lady extolling the virtues of a suburban optometrist).

"Hold on," she said, clicking the door shut on the way out. I wished she had left the door open so I could check out the other merchandise. How hard was it, really, to tell an aging whore that she's not your cup of tea? Seemed easy enough, but I just flat-out couldn't manage it.

A skinny white brunette with ghetto-style gapped teeth came through the door, dressed like a convalescent housewife in an outsized T-Shirt and tights. She wasn't pretty even in the dim, quote/unquote seductive light of the bedroom, but my heart skipped a beat nonetheless. She looked exactly like the kind of woman who'd find you if you were cheating on her, who would drag you out of the $22 a night motel you were holed up in with a girl from your office and beat you with a stick until your face was changed for the worse somehow.

"You didn't say nothing about a blonde. You just asked for Brittany. That's all you said." She spoke with obvious conviction, she could've been in a TV Movie of the week. If they ever made one about ugly call girls and their female pimps. I had a flash of me caressing one of her bony little feet and sucking the barely visible grains of salt from each of her toes, one by one.

"I'm sorry. I thought I did request a blonde. It must've been someone else I talked to, another place I called." Who would buy that shit? It was 11 on a Saturday morning – I couldn't imagine anyone else doing incalls until at least two or three on a weekend.

She smiled at me through taut lips. "You don't have to be sorry. If you ain't interested, you can just leave." I felt like I'd cheated her and Brittany somehow. A part of me just wanted to grab a couple of twenties and hand them to Brittany's business manager as a sort of kill fee. But her face was too hard, her manner too resolute and mannish. On my way out, I had this craving to put my fingers on her lower back, to pull her toward me and compel her to slow dance with me to the BeeGees' "How Deep Is Your Love?", which had just started playing on the aforementioned stereo.

When I got back out to my car, I checked my reflection in the mirror. I suppose I couldn't complain exactly – my stomach was rounded, but not obscene for my age; the gray in my hair actually looked more distinguished than superannuated; my face wasn't all that wrinkled (a good thing, really, considering all I'd been through lately). And when I wore a jacket and a tie, I got my share of admiring looks from women.

But all that is merely ballast, really, something I say to distract myself from the reality that I have no outlet on a Saturday morning and that two hundred dollars – two hundred! -- can't even buy a decent incall whore in Washington, DC.

There was nothing to do, really, but find a chair and drink. I drove out on 355 past Bethesda to one of my favorite bars, a little sports place called The Luckie Duckie. Cheap beer, good food, clean enough – The Duckie featured twentysomething women attired casually in translucently tight tee-shirts and suggestively clinging yellow shorts. There were rarely discernable panty lines. It was still a few minutes before noon, so the place was relatively quiet as I sat down for the first of what I hoped to be quite a few cold ones.

I sat down at the bar in front of a set mutely playing one of those teenage sitcoms where everyone lives in California, has good hair, and sports a deep, but not overbearing, tan. These shows were genius – this one I was watching I'd seen before, it was called *Surfer High*. They created an alternate teen universe, one in which the kids danced to synthesized-sounding pre-rock music. One in which the most popular, desirable kids in the school were "best buds" with the principal; in which the traumas and troughs of adolescence were glossed over/filtered out/distilled for children between the ages of six to twelve. There was no bulimia in Surfer High, no suicide attempts.

I watched the antics of Clark (the most popular, the alpha male, the one whose portrayer, Paul-Michael Dellums, would be reduced to commercials and supermarket ribbon cuttings after the series ended) at a school dance. He seemed to be having trouble deciding between Bethany (alpha female; sixteen my ass, not with those tits) and Leslie (pretty enough, wore glasses – so she must've been intellectual). I drank a couple, went to the bathroom. When I came back, the channel had been switched to ESPN. To some small college basketball game.

And the stool next to mine had become occupied. I could only assume said occupation was purposeful. I sized my *new drinking buddy* up: early thirties (going on forty-five – languid weekend afternoons at suburban fly-by-nights like this would seem to ensure premature aging); potbellied; faded tattoo on his arm. And his hair. Jheri curled (with a bald spot); a Fu Manchu mustache. He looked like the poster child for self-abasement, far too inherently tragic for satire. And he sought me out for companionship.

We talked. We talked in concentric circles, sticking to sports bar topics because we were in a sports bar. The Wizards would make the playoffs, only to get eliminated in the first round again. Too many glory hounds, too many prima donnas, he said. I voiced my opinion that perhaps they should sign Latrell Sprewell, just so maybe the coach would get strangled. Maybe a coaching change was their only hope, I amplified.

But he didn't catch on to the violence in my intonation, the raw unsteadiness inherent in my voice. Maybe he was just dumb as a post, maybe what I said hit too close to home. Perhaps my drinking buddy harbored his own fantasies of violence, for the sake of sweet retribution, or just because. Football. Football! The Redskins! Nine and Seven again! My acquaintance – not a friend, not even in the ultimately transitory atmosphere of Luckie Duckie's – thought a new lineman would make all the difference. He thought Sean Gilbert was worth nine million a year. Or whatever. Or maybe a new quarterback. I recognized the trouble with people like him; they always lurched towards the quick fix. Unhappy? Eat a box of doughnuts! Give your soul to Jesus Christ! Problems with your marriage? Start going to community education classes, meeting interesting people. Start spending inordinate amounts of time with these people. Leave your husband! Just leave a note, leave your son, file for divorce!

And he thought Sean Gilbert would solve it. He thought replacing Frerotte would ease the pain, would take our Skins deep into the playoffs. Maybe even to a division title in the watered down NFC East, where the mighty Cowboys had grown grizzled, old, and fat, where the Giants – God help us all – could win a division title. The problem wasn't a player. It wasn't a coach. It was the atmosphere of DC itself. At night, I cruised the city. I knew the desolation of Southeast, the NIMBY shortsightedness of Georgetown and Glover Park. I knew how the Hispanic ghetto of Cardozo seethed with the gangrene of underachievement. I'd seen the bleakness on the faces of the troupes of gay men exiting their haunts in Dupont Circle and Adams Morgan. It was because of all of these things, and a zillion other factors besides, that there would be no success stories in RFK, in Jack Kent Cooke. The *DC Metropolitan Area* was vitiated, as cursed as a pillow pissed on by an old dog. The young hoodlums of Wheaton, of Annandale and Silver Spring, could never truly "represent" as I've heard them say; their Foot Locker-bought replica jerseys would always reek of institutionalized mediocrity and credit-card debt, passed down from generation to generation like sickle-cell anemia and low-grade depression.

I didn't say any of this to my partner in conversation. He would not understand. I thought of my dad, dead at fifty-five after tumbling down icy steps after imbibing a six-pack. I had dreams when I was younger of him initiating his fall, of voluntarily launching himself. And even now.

I first saw them in the mirror above the bar: a couple, in their early twenties (just a few years older than my boy), sitting on the same side of a booth's bench seat eating Buffalo wings. Every so often they would tongue kiss, they would stop eating to dab crumbs or sauce off of each other's mouths with napkins. Moments like that eluded me, even when I was dating my ex-wife; Lydia didn't seem to have time for those types of games, and I was a bit more direct when I wanted her. All that flirting stuff was cute, I supposed, but pointless. Ancillary to satisfaction of my needs, you could say.

My son was my polar opposite. I left my porno magazines and my erotic playing cards in the most obvious of all obvious quote/unquote hiding spots; the bottom of my underwear drawer. The materials went unmolested. He never tampered with *any* of my things; never messed with my razor and shaving cream until he'd begun sprouting facial hair, never messed with my car until licensed to drive. And he never let me tell him what men were and what women were. And he refuses, to this day, to discuss his mother with me.

BACHELOR FATHER

I patted my hair into shape – theoretically speaking – all the while placing the full bore of my concentration on the young couple in the mirror. The $495 a month rent on a one BR/one bath couple. The two job boyfriend couple: the couple with the girlfriend who bitched and moaned to mom and aunts; who gamely hid bruises with long-sleeve shirts and a judicious use of pancake makeup. Who listened to the comfortably sterile Trisha Yearwood/Vince Gill new country on her way to cashier at Giant, Safeway, Shoppers' Club. This existence was hard and cold and perfectly normal; I could understand it. If he were my son, I would tell the man in the mirror that I know how you fall in traps like this. I would tell the girl that I know he takes out his frustrations on you. I made him and I'm sorry. I'll try to reason with him, but he's so hard, really. He's just like his old man.

But these people had no connection to me. And my son, he wouldn't even play this tawdry game of premarital cohabitation, of fucking housewives he met while delivering paint for Sherwin-Williams, of getting drunk and fucking shit up and making his return to the scene of his crimes a de facto apology. My son acted positively and reacted judiciously. He was a boarder I didn't really know.

I pulled up to my spacious, 3 bedroom, 2 ½ bath ranch style home and heard the unbearable thumping mechanized beats coming from within. My son was home, and it was the weekend. My son, who inexplicably chose me over the image, the ideal of his departed mother and who spent all of his money and time on music and retreats with his friends. I opened the door and the vocals and the rhythm and the tacky keyboards assaulted me. Over and over, the shrieking of 'Jesus is the way – J-j-j-j-Jesus is, Praise, Praise, Praise!'. My son – a club kid for Jesus.

He must have heard the door. "Dad! I'm in the kitchen heating up a pot pie – you want one?"

"No, Tommy – I want you to turn that crapola down! I can't hear myself think." I looked down the hall through the open doorway of his bedroom, his empty virginal bedroom with its glossy posters of Carman and DC Talk, the vacuous airbrushed pin-up boys of fundamentalist pop culture. "I want to talk to you, son."

Tommy walked into the room amiably enough, drinking HI-C from a drink box. I know I should've been thankful; rather than emotionally collapsing from the onus of my myriad emotional collapses, my public drunkenesses and my banal sobriety – all my glib, desultory advice! – *my boy persevered*. He didn't turn to drugs. He didn't drop out of school for a job at a hardware store and feral sex with girls with raincoat-yellow fingernails. Not Tommy. Tommy instead turned to community service, to drug-free get togethers with like-minded teenagers. He was a negation of everything I stood for and believed in, and affirmation of all I knew enough to renounce -- and I hated him for it.

"What's up, Dad?" Tommy smiled at me and I felt subtly mocked. It was all I could do to look my own son in the eyes.

"Nothing… son." I solved the problem of looking at him straight on with that old speech class technique of looking slightly above his head. The corners needed dusting.

"So, what are you doing tonight? Saturday night, huh?" I clapped my hands together and heard my question and my clapping resonate through the living room, so much emptier since Lydia moved her mother's antiques and her 'library furnishings' out.

"Yeah, dad! Carrie's coming over --"

"Oh, Carrie!" I laughed. They'd been seeing each other for about six months by then, and I strenuously hoped that either hormones or social pressures would take their course on my boy, would lead him from the arena of furtive white-knuckle chastity to guilty premarital sex on my bed when I wasn't home. "What do you two lovebirds intend to do?"

"Tonight we've got some plans you might enjoy, Dad. We're having a sort of impromptu Audrey Hepburn film festival."

"Audrey Hepburn, Tommy? What the hell…" I really didn't understand my son in the slightest. "Why don't you get Trainspotting or Fargo or something? I read about those movies – they're supposed to be really challenging." What is your obsession with the brittle, sexless past, I wanted to ask him.

"Oh, dad!" Tommy punched my arm, like men do in sports deodorant commercials. "Carrie has never seen Breakfast At Tiffany's, can you believe that? So we're going to get that…"

I tuned out for a bit. Give or take a week, it had been nine months since the divorce with Lydia went through. For what it's worth, the divorce was all her idea and doing; all I did was not stand in her way. I got cocky. I thought I wouldn't miss her. I thought she'd come back. Neither was the case – it turned out solitude suited her in ways that married life with me never could.

"Oh, one more thing, Dad?" Tommy's face went serious, and I didn't know what he was going to ask me. "About tonight. Carrie wishes you'd watch the movies with us. If you have other plans, that's fine. But it would mean a lot to her."

I seriously doubted that was Carrie's idea. Ever since Tommy found religion, I had become his number one reclamation project. He had put every bottle in my liquor cabinet outside for the trash men one day, like it undoubtedly said for him to do in some temperance pamphlet. He ran the gamut of intervention techniques, rarely losing his temper or raising his voice. Deep down within, I never came to trust it. His whole approach to my psychology was unbearably naïve – Tommy had overlooked how much I had always hated everything and everybody I came in contact with.

"Tommy… we'll see. I might have some plans that I can't get out of. Let me make some calls."

I lay down on what was once the conjugal waterbed, drawing the satin sheet over my face like a veil. I was intimately acquainted with Lydia's new number, calling it more often as time passed, usually hanging up before someone answered. Sometimes I waited too long and had to hang up on her. Once or twice I had to hang up on a husky-voiced man with a European accent.

I let the phone ring thrice, four times, and then the machine picked up with its terse, businesslike greeting. "Hello, this is Lydia De Wit." *No longer Lydia Brandi, no longer my wife* I caught myself thinking. "I'm not available to take your call at the moment, but I'd be delighted to return your call – that is, if you leave your message at the beep." I could hear the dual tinklings of light, social laughter and windchimy New Age music in the background. I wondered if Lydia had found her inner strength within, while not quite overcoming my darkest fear that she was an inveterate call screener. But I took the risk anyway, talking to her machine even while I was sure that she could be fearing me or taking a perverse satisfaction in my awkward message leaving skills. I was classically passive-aggressive; during the waning days of our marriage, she had rightfully learned to be wary of me at anytime that I wasn't sleeping.

"Uh, Lydia. Hi! It's me, Thurston. Well, of course you know that it's me… I thought I'd see what you were up to tonight, maybe invite you over to watch a movie with me, Tommy, and his girlfriend. We're watching Audrey Hepburn, if you can believe that."

I paused for a second, then started talking again, quickly. I feared getting cut off without being able to close the message in a way not immediately evocative of a deep-seated personality disorder. " I remember how you used to love Audrey Hepburn…" My voice trailed off, just for a second. I had intended to laugh socially soon thereafter. But the machine had heard enough. It beeped, terminating my connection.

By the time I came out of my bedroom, Tommy's girlfriend had already come over with the videos in tow. She had set them decorously between Tommy and herself on the sofa. "You'll have to go on without me tonight, kids – I couldn't shake my plans!" I called out from the hall.

They said something back that registered vague disappointment. I could've just seen myself on their movie date, sitting in between them on the couch watching Funny Face, Carrie patting my arm intermittently to let me know she liked me and that I was important to her because I was important to my son. I wasn't ready to be treated like a senior citizen just yet, I figured. I was still in the prime of my life.

I ambled out to my car, watching the old couple next door eye me suspiciously, as they had ever since Lydia left. The old woman thought the world of her. I believe the old man was sleeping with her. I waved in their general direction and got in my car, started it, and turned the radio to an anonymous college basketball game just to block out the thoughts in my head.

BACHELOR FATHER

I was no longer married to my special girl, my Lydia who binged when things were good and purged otherwise, who fasted away her myriad grievances, who consumed enough Slimfast and lite beer to make future cancer a certainty. I had returned to bachelorhood, newly wed to bachelor things – sports bars and Saturday night cruises down fast-food drive-thru lanes and the flirting, *always the flirting*, with the cashier, the waitress, the hostess. But sometimes I saw something better, something that fit the true me, the one that only existed on old home movies and in the boxed-away photo albums. Sometimes I wanted to howl.

I didn't stop to straighten my tie, to make sure my socks' argyles were correctly aligned. I had determined instead to leave estranged wives in the distant past where they belonged.

I drove down to Dupont Circle in the heart of the city and found an open bar – not a sports bar, but a self-styled "meeting place for attractive singles." It was Old Wave night; in the background, "Tainted Love" by Soft Cell played for the entire assembled throng. Meanwhile, I held a stool at the bar, downing whiskey sours and leafing desultorily through a discarded Post sports page, clucking sagely and anonymously at the recounts of recent Caps and Wizards losses. I felt the brushing of women against my back, women aerobicized firm, the brushing of lamb's wool and cotton and silken blends.

And as so often happens when a man is alone in a place like this, he eyes a woman who is just pretty enough, yet accessible enough for him to have a chance with. My girl was at the other end of the bar, sipping something with orange juice in it. Maybe a vodka drink, maybe a gin drink. I wasn't sure.

I looked her over throughout all of "Relax" and the better part of The Power Station's "Some Like It Hot", studying her slender frame, her beautiful office-worker hands, impeccably manicured no doubt by an anonymous nail tech in one of those Vietnamese manicure/pedicure places that have sprouted of late like so many mushrooms. Her Adam's Apple was a bit large, but nothing I couldn't live with. She was someone I could see taking Lydia's place in some small way. Maybe the introductory Sunday brunches at local restaurants would eventually give way to something else – pancake breakfasts in bed on drizzly Sunday afternoons as I read the Book World over her shoulder. I wasn't sure what. But I was willing to stick around to find out.

"Stuck With You" by Huey Lewis and The News was playing, and everyone in the bar – except for me, of course, plotting a revision of my very destiny – had settled into a relaxed conviviality in keeping with the mid-tempo soft rock hit. I had drank quite a few by then, stood up, and found myself staggering into clumps of women, clumps of men, all of them talking and making plans. I felt bile rising in my throat and swallowed it back – my more visceral urges could wait. *The room was moving, people were all making plans.*

I sidled up to her at the bar. "Bartender, give her another of whatever she's having, why don't you?" She smelled of White Shoulders and of a particularly resonant hair gel.

"Let me introduce myself," I said, hitching up my pants. "I'm Thurston Brandi. I've been noticing you from across the room – did you see me over there?"

Behind her, in a smoky haze, a couple was kissing. A man and a woman whose naked forms undoubtedly fit together perfectly under the cover of night on Outer Banks beaches. *I could see them kissing.* I moved closer to my anonymous companion.

"Hi, Thurston. I'm Talitha. I didn't notice you at all." I felt her arm graze against my torso. To my right, I noticed a girl I dated briefly – Effie Dumbarton – writing her name and number in Sharpie marker on a cocktail napkin for a new acquaintance. She was so old, he was so young. They would have been so young. I had a chance with Talitha, I just knew it.

The song had changed. Psychedelic Furs' "Pretty In Pink" filled the room, and even though Talitha was wearing black it seemed to be a fine song for my proposed seduction. Another mid-tempo rock number, another singer bleating about existential despair yet somehow – maybe it was the odd major chord here and there in the song – the tune left me with a sense of hope.

"So, *Thurston*, what do you want?" She shifted her body on her stool, newly staring me head on. She was fierce and mercurial and passionately grim, another DC office worker fighting gray hairs and the inevitable encumbrance of her father's Hoffaesque body type.

"Sorry, sorry, sorry. I just wanted to talk to you, is all." I smiled in her general direction, feeling myself starting to collapse under the weight of all the intrabar conversations, the proposed kisses and promises of furtive beddings and kvetches about office politics, all of the can you believe what Harper did and I'll pay for half, just don't bother me with the details and the I'm going to have to leave her you or I would ever want to hear. My sweat smelled of cured pork, the swine of bacon and fatback, and I felt my veins popping out of my forehead and my arms. I could feel an aneurysm beginning to build.

I reached out for Talitha's shoulder. I wanted to touch her, to let her know that there were times I wasn't like this. That I was getting a little bit old, maybe, but that I could see us together perhaps. I reached out for her; she shrunk back, and my hand grazed the front of her chest. She wasn't wearing a bra.

The seduction went awry. Talitha started kicking at my shins, my thighs, the pelvis – all my nether regions fair game, and it wouldn't be sporting to block. She was a girl. Then I noticed a new song fade into the old wave mix ("The Different Story"; Peter Schilling), and a group of apparent regulars took turns beating the hell out of me until the staff intervened, pulling them off of me, showing me the exit in very specific and direct terms.

I walked the neighborhood streets aimlessly for a while after that. I studied my cuts in the reflections of shop windows, my bruises and lacerations lending my face a certain seriousness. I tailed a woman for a couple of blocks. When she noticed, when she turned around, I gamely smiled at her. She looked away, ducked into a seemingly random Starbucks, apparently secure in thinking that she could do better than an aging, paunchy accident victim. I considered hitting her up for change, but then thought better of it. It wasn't exactly my lucky day, and I was getting a distinct feeling my days of low-grade sexual intrusion were going to come to an end. Maybe, they had to come to an end. Maybe someone would actually take the initiative and call security sometime sooner than later. In any case, my fellow passenger wasn't a chance I was willing to take that night.

I staggered toward my vehicle. I could barely stand up, and I tasted the saline warmth of my own blood, all the while feeling the concussion's intoxicating lightheadedness. God only knew what was dislodged, what was missing. Then I heard Tommy's voice echoing through the deserted residential street behind me.

"Dad! Yoo-hoo! Over here!"

I turned to look at my son, letting my abrasions and contusions stand as a self-indictment.

"Dad! What happened to you?"

Insert a moralistic phrasing here. Insert the obligatory "Oh, I was messin' where I shouldn't have messed." Give him a moral to seeing his father looking like a skid row bum, so he'll learn something from this harrowing experience. Impart a tidy little lesson about the evils of sexual desire run amok. Or not. "I got mugged…two bigassed Samoans… where are you and Carrie off to? So late."

"We were headed to the J.C. Disco. DJ Testament is playing – but never mind that! Dad – we're taking you home…"

No questions asked about where I had went. Not even the slightest allegation of moral turpitude from my son or his girlfriend. Just acceptance, always acceptance. And love. And tolerance. For one night, I would accede to his wishes. I would come home with him and let him put ice packs on my bruises and spackle over the pock-marks of my life with the blandishments of cable tv ecumenism. I'd read the sections of the Saturday paper I hadn't touched – Metro, Real Estate, TV Week – and maybe watch some mediocre sketch comedy before going to bed. For this one night, I would keep up appearances and stay home, thinking of my son, who would've kissed those illusory Samoans on their cheeks.

(3) Cutter

I remember how it was right before I discovered Exacto blades for myself. I was in seventh grade and I was failing everything, mostly because I didn't do my homework and skipped classes to go play video games at the Korean grocery across the street. There was no reason to stay in school anyway – I didn't have any girls crushing after me the way they did all the popular rich boys from the security gated subdivisions – Otranto, Aspen Hill, Belvedere – at the other end of town. The last time I went home I looked at some pictures and it was my unintentionally "retro" wardrobe that did me in, I think: my K-Mart clothes that were passé even in 1983; my butterfly collars and my corduroy flares. I never did the couples' skate at the skating rink. I just hung out by myself, watched, and played Galaga, kicking the machine whenever I died.

I was in my room beating all hell out of a Raggedy Andy doll I stole from my cousin's house and I heard my dad call out from across the house asking me if I wanted anything from McDonald's or Wendy's, he had to go get gas and would pass by there anyway. I told him no thank you. I'd learned to respect my elders after a series of lessons from my dad involving everything from belts and switches to water torture and standing still with my arms outstretched holding out gallon jugs of water till my arms completely gave out. I waited until I heard the Camaro cough its way out of the driveway before I gave Raggedy Andy another crushing piledriver.

Then it hit me. What I was doing was really stupid. I was thirteen years old and playing with doll babies. I threw Andy into my closet, watched him crumple and sag amidst the bowling balls and the dirty clothes in the floor. He looked like I'd snapped his spine. I punched myself in the forehead, but I didn't feel much so I punched myself harder, put more knuckle into it. Then I saw the bright flash of white light that comes when consciousness is interrupted somehow. I punched myself a third time, staggered off the bed, went into the bathroom, and puked. After that I played Centipede on my Atari.

Soon after that, this girl moved into the neighborhood. I stared out of the front door's peephole and watched her ride her bicycle around and around my circle, her hair windswept against her skull, her cheeks red like she had heat stroke. I saw her sitting by herself on the school bus, sometimes, and watched her through the security mirror staring out of the window towards the industrial parks and occasional gas station on the way to my school, Free Man Consolidated Middle.

One morning I got up from where I was and I went to where she sat and sat down. The whole back of the bus Oooh!'ed collectively and Vin Righter, the token fifteen-year-old 8th grader, said what was on everybody's mind, "Oh shit! Little Faggot Jimmy's got a girl-friend!" Vin got up and did a mincing strut with hand flourishes, and grabbed his dick through his camouflage pants. All the girls back there with him – Priscilla Dock, the D-Cupped cheerleader who would be knocked up and dropped out of school within a year; Tami Tipton, perhaps the most feared female bully in the entire school, a sixth-grader who'd fuck you up as soon as look at you – let out throaty laughs.

I sat there next to her and I didn't know what to say. I couldn't even look at her. I could smell her though, she had this wicked perfume on, almost sickening-sweet, so different from the Charlie my mother would spritz on herself before she went to her job in the meat department at the Winn-Dixie. I immediately regretted my decision. I wanted her to turn and talk to me – would it have been so hard, really? – she had everything.

When we got to school, I made sure I was the last to get off the bus. I sat there in my seat, alone, feeling around in my back pack, just passively watching as Vin Righter clocked this chick's phone number. It was Tuesday morning. It was sixty-eight degrees, and clouds were looming to the west. The air smelled like fertilizer and bus exhaust.

I had taken enough crap on the normal part of the school bus for that week, so I cut my losses and rode in the front with the retards, the kids who before the budget cuts had had their own short bus to take them to school, mongoloids and people who stuttered and people who couldn't walk in a straight line. Was I one of them? Was I just as fucked? I knew people said things about me, but I also knew that I was too chickenshit to do anything about it.

That Friday I skipped school, claiming to be sick to my stomach. I cut at least once a week, it wasn't like anyone called me on it. At 11:00 I turned on Little House On The Prairie and ordered a large cheese pizza from Domino's, paying for it twenty minutes later with rolls of nickels and pennies. The driver, a short, balding man that smelled like an egg roll, smiled at me and chuckled softly as he told me never to order from him. I screamed fuck you at him after I closed the door, after he was back in his Dodge Omni listening to ZZ Top's "Velcro Fly" as high as his stereo would go. Fuck you, chink link, I screamed because he was Chinese and because my dad was in Vietnam and had taught me the difference between a chink and a gook.

At 11:52 I turned up the tv as loud as it would go, went into the bathroom, and gagged up the pizza during an Ed McMahon commercial for life insurance for people aged 50 to 80. Nobody could be turned down, and there was no obligation. Most of the pizza was still in solid chunks. It tasted much the same coming back up, though maybe the tomato sauce was a little more acidic. At 12:15 I rode my Huffy dirt bike down to the 7/11 and bought a box of powdered mini-donuts and a Big Gulp Mello Yello. The air hung heavy and wet, smelling of pine trees and garbage.

I pedaled around my neighborhood as fast as I could after I ate my food in front of the 7/11. I imagined I was in that movie about the guy with no legs who bicycled across Canada. I liked to pretend I was in one movie or another as someone who was overcoming a bad hand God or Mother Nature dealt him. But it was hard to be a sacrificial, heroic figure when you had hiccups.

I took a different turn than I usually did, into this trailer park that my mother always told me not to go in, it was overrun by potheads and niggers. But I felt defiant, somehow, like even if there were potheads and niggers and child molesters in white vans I could kick their asses. I slowed down as I entered though, breathing the metallic, melancholy air in more deeply, staring pensively at the municipal power station about 100 feet to the left of the entrance and relaxing, somehow, to the reassuring hum of the generators.

The trailer park was deserted. I expected hookers on corners and men in trenchcoats signaling that they had something to sell – that was how it was on filmstrips in Health And Community class after all, black women with afros looking like Pam Grier and black men looking like Isaac Hayes, with shiny, bald, black heads and fat gold chains – but there was nothing. The closest thing I saw was a parked gray van with tinted windows and an airbrushed desert scene on the side – a cactus, a cowboys wielding a lasso; a setting red sun.

I pedaled and coasted around the trailer park for another couple of minutes. There was no danger there. Just people even more raggedy than we were. A fat mongrel bitch tied to a doublewide's front steps licked herself desultorily. I could hear the saccharine strings of a soap opera's theme song blasting from a rusted out singlewide. Then I heard a girl calling my name.

I swiveled my head around. I had no idea where the sound was coming from.

"Jimmy – over here. To your *left*." I can't believe I didn't notice to start with. The girl from the bus was sitting face down on a towel in her front yard, barefoot, in a bikini top and jeans. We were alone except for the humming of the power station in the background. It was almost like a date.

"Do you live around here?"

"Un-uh, I live over there." I pointed in the general direction of my house, even though a fence, a four-lane road, some scrubby pines, and an abandoned brick warehouse with MEAT painted on it in fading, blocky, peach letters with brown outlines stood in between.

“Oh. Want to come inside? You’re sweating like a stuck pig.”

I nodded my head. I could see the outlines of her nipples through her bikini top, baby blue with palm trees, surfers, and ocean waves on it in a repeating print.

She sat me down on the day bed in her bedroom and told me to hold on a second, she had to go find something. I wondered if those were her sheets, her pillowcases I was sitting on. I wanted to lie down on them, to see if I recognized the smell. Would it be her perfume, or just that warm, familiar bedclothes smell of dead skin? At home, my pillowcases like cooled buttermilk biscuits; dandruff.

She turned her television set to MTV. A Flock Of Seagulls was playing.

“Hey. Sorry I didn’t say anything to you on the bus. It’s hard for me to talk to people first.” I was lisping. I tried to keep it in check. Sometimes I did exercises in front of the bathroom mirror. It helped occasionally to talk in a deeper voice, but I always slipped up sooner or later.

“I’ve seen your house,” she blurted out.

“Yeah, I know.” I didn’t tell her how many times I’d seen her riding by. I didn’t tell her I got the vibrating egg out of my dad’s dresser drawer and made up encounters for me and her after I saw her pedal by.

“I always see you on the bus, Jimmy, but you never talk to anyone. Don’t you want to talk to people?” Restating the obvious, she moved closer to me and kissed me on the neck. I froze up. I could feel her breast against my arm, and I shifted my shoulder into it.

“Do you like my room?” she asked, moving away from me. I nodded my head. It was a typically cramped bedroom in a single wide, crammed with a creaky, fake brass bed (in places the metallic gold paint was chipped off, leaving the dull, gray finish underneath exposed), a tiny worn-out writing desk that looked like it had been dug out of someone’s trash thirty years ago, and a thirteen-inch tv that was barely big enough to hold the cable box on top of it. There were three posters on the walls: one with tattered corners of a unicorn in a hazily green field; another, better-preserved – of a kitten lying in a basket of straw. The second poster had a caption. It said "Happiness is." The third was the only one that looked like she'd bought it in the last couple of years; a print of Steve Perry wearing tight jeans with a hole in the left knee, sitting side-saddle on a motorcycle. She reached under her bed and got out a pack of cigarettes and a lighter. She lit up and we both took drags.

"Yeah. Your room's pretty cool." I'd never smoked before, and I'd half expected to have one of those moments where I coughed and hacked like people did on television, but nothing like that happened. My mom and dad both smoked like they were racing each other to the cancer clinic, and I guess I'd gotten used to it that way.

She went to her desk and got out a spiral notebook with Brainy Smurf on the cover. She came back, sat down, and put her hand on my upper thigh, firmly, like she was trying to sell me some insurance. "What's my name, anyway, Jimmy?"

"I don't know."

"What do you mean? I know yours."

"Yeah, you know Vin Righter's too, I'll bet," I muttered to myself.

"I'm *Ursula*," she said, in a way that suggested I was supposed to think it was a pretty goddamn cool name or something. I wondered if she noticed my erection. I wanted to hide it with a pillow, but there was no way I could move without disrupting the situation.

She excused herself momentarily. I picked up her notebook and looked at what she'd done to Brainy's face. She'd cut his forehead. The notebook's cover was, like, ventilated. I looked over at her desktop's assortment of dust-covered crap. A crimson, leatherette jewelry box; a 6x9 mirror like you'd win at the fair with Quiet Riot's logo in the bottom right hand corner; a pocket-sized copy of the New Testament, the kind they give you on your first day of Sunday School when you've been brought to church charity-case style by a family who actually belonged to the flock. I had one of those Bibles myself.

Ursula took her time coming back in, and when she did she was brushing her teeth. She was one of those really vigorous teeth brushers, spittle was bubbling out of her mouth, paste speckling her baggy black t-shirt. "Wanareama noboke."

I looked at her kind of cockeyed. "What?"

She left the room, spit, and came back. "Do you want to read my notebook?"

I just looked at her, dumbly, a tourist without a clue where to go.

"I have to change."

I looked down at the floor.

"Either leave or turn your head."

The closest thing to sex for me – the rustles of her bikini top and jeans being shed and dropped on the floor, new clothes coming on, a muffled burp. I pulled my shorts over my stomach, tweaked my nipples so my pecs wouldn't hang all flabby. My dad had started telling me I had titties.

I turned around. She was adjusting a tight T-shirt that hugged her breasts and some shorts. Her thighs were striated with rows of intricate scars highlighted by the occasional fresh slash.

"What are you staring at?" I wasn't quite sure if she even knew what her legs looked like.

"Ursula… what happened to you?"

"Nothing. Nothing – at – all." Even as she let out a deep, loud breath, her eyes looked at me, daring me to ask her another question.

"But why?" I could hear myself starting to whine. I sucked up some phlegm to deepen my voice. "I mean, Ursula, you realize it's harmful, right?"

She looked at me, laughing quietly and oozing a deep-seated contempt.

"Yeah. What's your point? You better leave now."

I suddenly felt a real fear for the first time since I'd seen her. "Wait. I'm sorry. I just never saw that before."

She took another deep breath and stood up, grabbing my hand, telling me to come sit by her. She picked up her spiral notebook and started reading.

"Death… like destruction's sun rays… pleasure is gone… I've lost you. Wait . . . no, not that one. It sucks." She flipped through the notebook's pages.

"Oh, here's a better one – I wrote this a couple of days ago. I saw the sad – I saw the sadness in all of their faces. Funerals take us all to bad places… There is no hope, no time to hope… I want to die, I want to –"

Her body was warm and she was breathing heavily. Ursula wasn't stuttering but she sounded nervous when she talked. Then we heard three knocks on the door, as loud as bricks hurled against aluminum siding.

"Oh shit. Get inside." She pointed at the closet door. Ursula turned off the television, then pushed me into the closet and slid the door most of the way shut. I knew what was coming next.

I heard a male voice, loud combat-bootsteps, Ursula giggling. This was the way my mom sounded when I went to see her and her boyfriends brought her home from a night drinking and breakfast at Huddle House afterwards. This was how my dad's tricks would sound after they and my dad smoked some dope in his bedroom with the door closed.

I'd never seen the guy before – must've been a high school guy, I guessed. He had a long, curly rat tail and the room all of a sudden smelled cheap and dirty, like dead cigarette smoke and dated sweat.

They talked some bullshit. He put her in a big bearhug and dipped her low to kiss her. They kissed, he released, and she staggered away, bumping into the stereo and turning it on. "Love Plus One" by Haircut 100 started blaring and Ursula's boyfriend called out, "Hey, turn that shit off. I've already got a fucking headache."

Ursula did as she was told. She grabbed him by his shirt collar and pulled him down onto the bed, on top of her, between her splayed legs. The bed creaked ominously, the cheap box springs sounding like they wanted to give completely. She grabbed his ass. They started kissing.

Eventually the shirts came off. His back was bony and pale with full, crimson pimples and old scars. Ursula's tits sagged and she had stretch-marks on her stomach which I somehow didn't notice outside in the bright Lowcountry trailer-park sunshine. No blowjobs, no sex. Just dryfucking. And even though the pants came off, the underwear was never removed. I could still hear the power plant humming tonelessly outside whenever they'd slow down or stop for a minute.

"Hey, I gotta go."

"Why? You never stay. Once you come, you go home."

He lit his cigarette and looked as contemplative as a person possibly can in dingy white briefs and gray sweatsocks. "I'm not going home. I've got to go to work. Got called in today."

"Goddamnit." For the first time pretty much, I realized how much older Ursula was than me.

"Goddamn yourself. I've got to head out now." He said this pulling his pants back on. "Want a ride somewhere?"

"I guess I'll stop by the mall." They got dressed and kissed some more and she left me in her bedroom closet without even saying goodbye. I found some rolls of change in another bedroom and some Star Crunch in a kitchen cabinet, and took them home with me.

I didn't even want to go to the skating rink the next day. But I got roped into it. My dad's brother, Melvin, was in town and had brought his son Teddy with him. Teddy was a real freak – he'd ask the same question four or five times and whisper your sentences back to you after you said them. He was always on the verge of getting slapped upside the head by someone.

So they dumped us off at the Rollerdrome. Watching Teddy get out of the back of a Ford Pinto was comic, I guess, in the way an overturned wheelchair is. First of all, he had the coordination of an upended turtle even when he wasn't crowded in, and when smushed into a closed space, some weird variation of claustrophobia took over where he started panting and drooling. He couldn't get comfortable in the back seat of a car, and I really hated his guts whenever I had to sit by him. One time I put a thumbtack down on the seat right before he sat down.

But not this time. I was still pissed off about Ursula. I got out and waited for Teddy and we walked into the skating rink, two pot bellied kids whose clothes were ratty and too small. I was wearing a muscle shirt with a cheetah airbrushed on the front, and looked down at my arms -- tiny whiteheads dotted the side of my biceps, and I absentmindedly pinched at them with my index and thumb nails.

Cutter

The rink was jumping. The floor was packed with all the cool kids doing tricks to "Love Is A Battlefield", pirouettes and speed-skating and whatever else. Johnny Reilly was weaving in and out of traffic, and knocked Brian Mills on his back. Brian looked like he had thought for a split second about doing something about it, but he instead grabbed the carpeted wall to pull himself to his feet and wobbled off the floor, nudging his glasses back on his nose.

Coming back from renting some skates, Teddy and I bumped into Ursula and the guy I'd watched her fuck a couple of days before. I tried to pull Teddy away, but he was obese and clueless and I was too clumsy on skates to escape from anyone anyway. The guy's hair was pulled back into a ponytail and he was wearing a black and gold satin warm-up jacket with a dragon on the left hand side.

"Jimmy!" she called out. They were both popping gum, and smelled like Bubblicious and old cigarette smoke. Teddy had sat down on the ground to retie his shoelaces. I tried to look like I wasn't with him.

"Hi, Ursula." I didn't know what to say to her.

"I was going to call you! I haven't seen you all weekend! What did you do?"

Well, I discovered masturbation. I found out that you should use Vaseline and not Noxzema. Lifted some candy from the convenience store. "Nothing."

"Just sat around, huh?" She furrowed her brow and nodded concernedly. "Have y'all met?" She looked at me and at the guy she was with. He looked me in the eye and I stared down at my shoes.

" I'm Todd. What's goin' on, man?" He had a deep voice.

"Hi, Todd. I'm Jimmy." I paused. "Nice to meet you." My voice was quavering a little bit. I got scared that he might say to me, "Hey, Jimmy, why don't we all three get the fuck out of here and go get some beers, maybe smoke some grass." What did I know? I was thirteen, and not even a cool thirteen. I was out of my league with Todd and his driver's license and his ability to make the girl of my dreams moan.

We talked some more bullshit for a minute or two. Teddy trundled off to the Pole Position machine and put his quarter in a row next to those of three or four other people who wanted next crack at the machine. Everyone wanted next.

"Vin-NAE! Over here, bro!" It was all over. I should've known that Vin Righter would show up. That Vin Righter would get in my business. Ursula smiled at him and Vin grabbed his cock and pointed at her. Todd asked him what was going on. Vin told him what was going on.

"Todd, what's this you're talking to?" He pointed at me. Ursula started talking to Tami Tipton, who I guess had come with Vin. "How 'bout I fuck him up!" He threw a punch at my face and pulled it about six inches from impact. I ducked and guarded anyway. He'd done this routine to me about twenty times in the previous couple of years, but never really hit me, just gave me a couple of smacks is all. I kept swearing to myself that one day I was going to hit him smack in the jaw. He was going to hit the concrete. I even had dreams about it sometimes.

"I'd like to see you try," I said quietly, kind of like I was asking to use the bathroom during a math test. I wasn't even convincing myself. "Prick."

Vin's eyes widened and his muscles tensed up. I didn't think in terms of everything in life being a soundtrackable moment then, but even if I had, I wouldn't have thought of "Caribbean Queen" by Billy Ocean as much of a fight song. Todd stepped between us just in the nick of time and held Vin back.

"Calm down, man. He's cool."

"I'll wipe his ass and send his mama the bill," Vin said. I actually calmed down then, instead of getting buck wild pissed the way most anyone else would've. Your mama jokes pretty much rolled off my back. I knew they weren't even half the truth. "Son of a bitch dickweed motherfucker wants to play --"

"Vin. Shut up already or I'll kick your ass myself." I had no idea why Todd was taking up for me. If this had been one of Vin's friends from our school, he would have been holding me while Vin slapped me until he got bored. "He's half your goddamn size, besides . . . " Todd pulled Vin over and started whispering in his ear. I couldn't make out anything he was saying but Vin laughed afterwards. Teddy still hadn't gotten his turn at Pole Position yet. They just walked away, all four of them, without saying anything to me. I played video games until the rink closed. I didn't even skate.

I skipped school for about the next week or so, and for some reason my dad let me get away with it. He had gotten fired or quit or something; for two or three nights in a row, we rode down to the place he drove for, Glascoe Trucking, and he searched the mailbox for a check they were supposed to leave for him. He said they weren't paying him, and he was tired of their shit, and he could fucking get a better job. "Shit, Jimmy, they pay me twelve cents a mile and they don't even make good on that and I talked to Rountree out in Summerville and he said he'd pay me sixteen-five on the spot whenever I wanted to come to work for him," he said. He made me check the mailbox myself, grabbing my arm and jamming it into the empty hole, telling me, "See? See?"

I gave him a roll of nickels for gas and a malt liquor. He'd pay me back, goddamn that pigfuck Glascoe. "Goddamn Glascoe," he said, pulling a healthy draw from the can, then throwing it – half-empty – at an old black lady pushing a boosted shopping cart that brimmed with empty plastic fast-food gimmick cups.

Both of us were home for Thursday, Friday, and a weekend. On Sunday evening he realized how ungrateful I was for all he'd done for me and shut me in the walk-in closet for a few hours to let me think about what I'd done. I waited till I heard the car pull out of the driveway and grabbed one of my mother's old paperbacks off the shelf. It was called "Lady Of Lace", and it was about an Georgia orphan who grew into a beautiful women just as the War Between The States erupted. Love eluded her, however, until the Yankees had burned down her modest farmhouse. As she sat by the side of the road, cold and scantily clad, a Confederate soldier rode by on horseback. He was dashing, strong, and tan, and took her to the safety of his mansion, which hadn't been touched by Sherman's marauders (they couldn't find it or something). I started crying, right there on the floor of the closet. I wanted to be rescued. I wanted to be saved. I couldn't finish the book.

Cutter

I rode my bike to school the next day. I showed up an hour and a half late without a note for my absences. After trying and failing to get a hold of my dad on the phone, they decided that it would be for the best if I went home and served a five day suspension. There were only so many times they could paddle me, after all.

I thought about riding over to my mother's house and asking her if I could stay for a couple of days while my dad sobered up. I hadn't been to see her in about a month. The last time I was there she'd had a new boyfriend and he and his daughter had moved in. She was six years old and scratched her head a lot, like she was trying to get at an itch below her skin. The boyfriend – Dillon – let his girl cuss my mother. He laughed, saying that the little girl had spunk. My mom wasn't quite as amused, but she was pushing forty and running out of options in her lovelife. She had to take what she could get, she told me when she took me home. She was a realist.

Fuck realism. I didn't care if I saw her again at this point, this woman whose trailer and car were corroding slowly, whose living room always smelled of mildewed carpet and dog shit. I rode back towards my dad's house, pretending the whole time that I was Darth Vader, fixing to abduct Princess Leia from Han-Solo and Luke Skywalker. I wanted to see all of them hurt very, very badly.

I rode right by my house when I saw my dad's car in the front yard. He had pulled up just about to the front door, like he always did after spending the night out. I didn't figure on going home for a while. Took some lefts, some rights, and stopped at the 7/11 for a Big Bite hot dog and a pint of milk. Unless I sucked in my gut, I could no longer see my feet.

I ate my food really quickly and got back on my bike. I felt bloated. I pedaled through stomach discomfort and acute indigestion. I turned left into the trailer park and didn't look around for apocalyptic signals. A scrawny middle aged man with a combover, wearing coach's shorts, flip-flops, and a baggy, dingy V-neck undershirt walked toward the rental office.

I found Ursula sitting on her front lawn, eating a Superstar ice cream popsicle. She didn't look surprised to see me.

"My hero," she deadpanned. Her hands were trembling.

"Your knee's bleeding. You ought to put a Band-Aid," I said. Her thighs were cut up; she'd been switched and there was even a bruise right below the hemline of her shorts, like she'd been hit with a book or something.

"No shit, Sherlock. Fat butterball retard." She choked out the last few words. Her face contorted into a scrunched, hateful mask, and she scampered inside, brandishing her melting popsicle in front of her like a torch in darkness. I dropped my bike and followed her into her house.

I sat beside Ursula on her bed and asked her what was wrong. She wouldn't look at me. She stood up, opened a window, and turned on a box fan.

"It smells like dirty feet in here," she said, pretty much out of nowhere. But it summed up the situation. "Why do you keep coming over here anyway? Nobody asked you to. You're such a loser – I guess you know that and all, you hear it enough, but it's really true. It's the only reason – besides being a faggot – that you'll never have a girlfriend. You'll never get out of here." She'd started crying again, loud, jagged sobs, the kind that make you start hyperventilating sooner or later.

"You're always going to live here in this stupid, tacky place. You're always going to have your mama around to buy you whatever you need. I know your type, Jimmy."

Her eyes were alight with fury and disgust. All the stuff that was on her desk before was gone. Who knew what had happened to the miniature Bible with the leatherette cover? The unicorn and the kitten had been consigned to the trashcan as well; the only thing on the wall was that poster of Steve Perry wearing tight jeans with a hole in the left knee, sitting side-saddle on a motorcycle.

(4) Lackey

Shana and I had made an arrangement. I would hang out with her and Mark sometimes. At her discretion. And if we did happen to go out to lunch or dinner together – the three of us – I was expected to put my customary stinginess on hold, to pay the check and tip adequately if not handsomely.

I agreed to all those conditions and several more besides. I could usually be counted on to do what was expected of me, at least as far as she was concerned. In many ways, after all, we were less best friends than master and supplicant.

She had had other lackeys before me, though she never titled any of them as such. There was the girl she met at a PreCollege program the summer before her senior year, a beautiful girl who, if the photographs were any indication, had but one handicap; one of those transistor-radio style hearing aids in her left ear. I never met this person, but I can imagine her duties: talking to her late at night after her dates, hearing Shana ask rhetorically if the guy was the one; going to the co-op on campus to buy her a consolatory Dove bar after a trying exam; occasionally brushing out her hair, maybe stroking her finger against the firm, yet delicate, wings of Shana's back, Shana's shoulders, as she combed out a particularly trying tangle (Shana's always had such difficult long hair). And if Shana's diary is at all believable, she shared other things with this girl, like her first girl-to-girl kiss, and other things roommates apparently do to relax each other. They were both sixteen, after all, and curious, and rooming behind the first locked doors that were truly theirs in their entire lives; they were both beautiful and had imaginations and knew enough to want the smooth curves and lines of each other's forms.

But this girl fell by the wayside, and there were the inevitable replacements. There were always replacements. The Mormon girl who lasted a few months. The Korean girl that Shana stopped calling out of utter boredom. The skinny Computer Science major that blew it when he and Shana were cuddling and he put his hand down the front of her panties for warmth. And then I, who had been waiting in the wings, going to movies by myself and issuing anathemas to my father and planning to move just as soon as I had the money, just as soon as I had the time; I who had been watching Shana's every move from afar, seeing her every so often at a party or someplace and exchanging distant smiles, came into my position.

She was gorgeous. I touched her every once in a while.

"So how long's he staying anyway?"

"Jesus, Jamie. Stop grilling me already. Maybe a week." She looked at me like I'd just eaten a roach.

"I'm not grilling you, I was just wondering, that's all. I'm sorry."

Shana kept looking at her magazine. "I'm sorry. I just, you know, wondered."

She didn't look up. She was waiting for me to shut my goddamned mouth. I eventually got the hint.

I skipped work that day to hang out with her, knowing it was the last time I'd be alone with her for days, even a week. I sat close enough to her on the couch that the hair on our arms bristled against one another, and I smelled her. She smelled like trees and Zest soap. She was wearing a black T-shirt from the Limited and some faded jeans she got for under twenty dollars at the used jeans store.

"So, should I just take the movies back, you know, when I leave?"

"No, Mark and I will take them back later." Her tone of voice was measured, as if she was restraining herself from saying something that might break me. I'd been nervous and skittish all day anyway (I always was when her boyfriends would come into town).

"So, Shana. I'm really sorry. I don't know why I'm acting like this and I wish I could quit. Okay?"

We shared about ten minutes of uncomfortable silence broken up only by my occasional apology. After we heard Mark knock on the door. Shana jumped up, and her face looked animated for the first time since I'd come over. She checked her lipstick and her hair – both perfect – in the reflection of the dormant tv, and I sat paralyzed on the spot. I wanted to have left already but I couldn't leave; I had to watch Shana interact with someone she loved.

It wasn't the kiss that bothered me (a deep, passionate soul kiss, in the midst of a hug that I'd never received from Shana who, when she did hug me, always approached even that with major reservations – her muscles would tighten like she was hugging a molesting uncle at a family reunion), but instead the things that came after the kiss. Mark's hand sifting her hair like it was sand on a beach, removing its mystic aura as he complimented her on its length ("your hair is longer… it looks really good"). The way Mark's hand would "accidentally" graze over her butt as he walked around her for some reason, and the way she didn't seem to mind his violations of her space at all. When Shana and I were alone, she was the untouchable, imperious object of all my attentions and concentrations, and was suffused with a haughty glamour; when she was with Mark, she showed an aspect of herself that I found entirely disturbing. She became a sucker for the cheap formulaics of courtship: their pet names ("Shani" and "Big Gun"); the way the caustic, haranguing edge went off her voice as she so sweetly told him stories about oddball customers who came into her work (she sold office supplies at an office supply store), about wacky things her parents said or did recently. We were in the same room, on the same couch, but I was alone and they were alone; Shana was sitting sideways on the couch, her back facing me, and even though her butt was flush against my leg, it wasn't enough to make me feel included. I was so peripheral!

I sat there and stared forward on Shana's couch, looking at her high school swimming team trophies and dusty pictures of her brothers and sisters. I brooded darkly, occasionally looking over to see if Shana was trying to make eye contact with me, if I was mistaken in thinking she was intentionally trying to ignore me. But it was no mistake.

Oh, Big Gun, I thought, if you could only know the way she'd treat you if you ever married her. Unlike Shani and Big Gun, I knew very well how inevitable it was that we disappoint the people whom we love. I saw it every day in my dealings with Shana, when she would send me home or hang up the phone in my ear in a fit of rage. She would be so disappointed, and I guess I was disappointed also, but my disappointment didn't matter so much. It never does when all you want is to be noticed.

After about ten more minutes of listening in to their conversation (traffic was heavy coming up the interstate… Shana had a freak run-in with a homeless person who was mildly rude to her… Mark preferred broiled chicken and fish over fried red meat), I made my excuses and my exit. I kissed Shana on the cheek as I exited, taking advantage of her good mood. And Mark and I had a test-your-grip sort of handshake in which we stalemated in trying to break each other's metacarpals.

I got home around twelve thirty and saw my dad once again proving he had no common sense whatsoever by pushing the mower across the front lawn in the afternoon sun. As my car became gradually more visible to him, he greeted me by pointing to the lawn and then shaking his fist menacingly in my direction. I cut the volume on my stereo and parked in front of the house.

He stopped his engine and glowered in my direction. "I told you to mow this two days ago!"

I didn't even look in his direction as I walked toward the garage. "Well, Dad, if you hadn't been watching Price is Right and Rush Limbaugh all morning, perhaps you wouldn't be out here getting heat stroke right now. Maybe you could've cut the grass before… never mind."

He took a deep breath. "All right, son. Your underwear and five dollars is on your bed."

I stopped and turned around to face him. "Oh yeah? You washed clothes?"

"What the hell do you think?" He yanked his cord and started the mower again and I finally made my way inside.

My father's house didn't totally look like a junk shop, although there were some resemblances. The shelves and tables were full of knickknacks he and my departed mother scavenged from the houses of their dead relatives. Little statuettes of puzzled-looking coal miners from the Kentucky branch of our family. Bookend Indians from some reservation in North Carolina. Dust-covered TV Guides here and there. And underneath a pile of debris was our answering machine blinking that we had two messages.

I pushed the button and collapsed on the couch with no real enthusiasm. "Jamie, it's Matt. Are you there, pick up. Oh, I guess not. Anyway, you know last night I went out with Stephanie, right?"

I knew Stephanie. The girl whose hips were wider than she was tall and who wore low-riding jeans with men's boxer shorts puffed over the waist like some kind of *cholita* or something. I'd wanted to sleep with her for about a year or so, but had never gotten around to it. Or something like that.

"So I go to her house and I'm going to pick her up, right? And I knock on her door and Keith answers…"

Three things: Keith was Stephanie's stepdad, or at least the man her mother was shacking up with; Stephanie was 16; Matt and I both were 21.

"Anyway, Keith starts in, pushing me and saying 'goddamnit, you child molester, we'll get a restraining order on your sorry ass', and I tell him, 'oh, okay, you'll stop me seeing Stephanie over my dead body, you motherfucker', and then he comes out with a baseball bat, and I'm like thinking that, yeah, you fat little fucker, you're going to need that bat, you know what I'm saying…"

I really didn't know what Matt was saying. I didn't know when he'd turned into a gangsta. I thought back a few months to when we went to the Midnight Madness at the county fair and these guys who looked like goddamn Boys II Men came up from behind him and pushed his face into the nachos he was eating as he walked. He didn't do shit. I figured that if Keith had really come out of his house with a bat, Matt would've probably run like hell. I started ignoring his voice droning on, turning my attention to last Sunday's sports section.

"... so, anyway, you should call me, and we'll go bowling or something. I haven't heard from you lately, and, well, you know. I'll be at Ricky's until four. Call me there."

I considered calling him, maybe. I picked up the cordless and laid it next to me on the couch. I waited for the next message to play, figuring it was from work or something.

"Jamie? Are you there? Guess not. This is Shana. Mark and I wanted to see if you'd come over and meet us for lunch. Call me. Bye."

The last two sentences had a lilt almost of promise, of suggestion. I had left her apartment thirty minutes before, disgusted with everything in my life beyond the breaking point, but was willing to forgive and forget at the first sign of Shana's slightest effort. Such is the way of the believer, the person who chases impossible dreams.

I immediately called her back and the phone rang three or four times. I hung up. Could they have left without me? I wanted to drive back over there, but I didn't want to seem any desperate than I already did, so I just kept calling every couple of minutes, filling the time between my calls with such interesting diversions as brushing my teeth, eating a poptart, and vacuuming the area around the bird cage. After the fifth phone call I left a message on Shana's machine.

"Hey, I just got your message. Yeah, sure, I'd be interested in lunch. Maybe I'll just... um, well, wait . . . I'll just call you back in a couple of minutes or you can call me back or something. Whatever, talk to you soon. Bye."

I turned around and punched the wall, watching the picture frame above where my fist had landed rock precariously. Not too long before that – a few days before – I had punched a hole in my bedroom wall, and it was only my father's abject disinterest in my affairs that saved me from him discovering said hole and kicking the shit out of me.

I had a system worked out for times like this. I turned on the Weather Channel and used the clock at the bottom of the screen to space out my calls. Every three minutes, I'd hit redial, and hang up on the machine. After the sixth try, Shana finally picked up.

"Hello," she called into the phone. I could hear her shower and Mark singing Primus' "Jerry Was a Race Car Driver" showtune style in the background.

"Hey, sweetie! Can I take you to lunch?" I was trying to be in a good mood, to invoke a feeling of levity, to create a conversational lift.

"Lunch? We're in the shower, Jamie!"

"Well, I was just returning your call…"

"Jesus, Jamie. Stop sounding like a whipped dog. 'I was just returning your call'. God, I'm sick of you."

I closed my eyes and thought of happier times with Shana. Sometimes she and I would have these conversations in which she'd insist that her haranguings were just aberrations. But if you put enough aberrations together they become their own pattern.

The singing had stopped. I called out Shana's name, but all I could hear was running water, giggling, and threats of sex. I knew their torsos were touching. I had prostrated myself in so many ways for just a small taste of what Mark had in his mouth. I had gotten out of bed at three in the morning to drive an hour into the nothingness out on I-10 to jump start that girl's car after her own parents, her own girlfriends, her own boyfriend told her to get a motel, they'd be there in the morning. I'd let her go through my closet and dump clothes she'd developed an aversion to. I'd stolen money from my own father's wallet so I could take her someplace decent for dinner, so I could even buy her roses once or twice (I was not rich by any means, even when I was working). So I stopped listening. I hung up my phone, went into my bedroom, and tried to make myself cry for ten or fifteen minutes.

She called me back after I'd managed to distract myself with a box of Twinkies, a can of Mountain Dew, and Final Fantasy VII. "When I got back on the phone, you'd already hung up, so I figured your dad had to use it or something."

"I sat there for *five minutes*, Shana."

"Jesus, Jamie, shut up already. I just told you I was sorry."

"Oh, okay, Shana. Sorry. I…"

I waited for her to ask me what.

"Shana, I know you need time alone with Mark, and all that. Why don't you just call me when, you know, he goes back home?"

"I don't think that's a good idea."

"Why? All you've done all day, in fact, all you've done for the last couple of weeks is push me away. Don't you think I get tired of it?" I remembered the 'don't you think I get tired of it' line from one of the last conversations my mother had with my dad, and thought it was a bit hokey, but somehow transcendently dramatic.

"Jamie, goddamn you. You push yourself away. Next you're going to tell me that Mark somehow slighted you. You need to stop acting like such a mincing little faggot."

"Okay. Okay." She'd won, again. "I'm sorry. I'll make it up to you… do you still want to go get lunch?"

"Hold on…" She didn't cover the mouthpiece, at least, but I still couldn't understand what they were saying. I considered her options as I waited for her. Despite my feelings for her, I knew full well that there wasn't anyone else she could – or would – hang around with. With her other friends she had to try to be entertaining, to try to make the friendship work. With me, all she had to do was sit back, take her shoes off, and relax. So basically whenever she stopped cursing me I knew we had plans.

"Okay. Jamie?"

"Yeah?"

"Why don't you just bring some stuff over from Home Cooked."

"Sure! What can I get for you today," I asked, as unctuously as any chain restaurant waiter.

"All right, I want the grilled chicken sandwich – no mayonnaise – and an order of mixed greens. Oh, and get a cheesecake too. And Mark wants the grouper steak with a baked potato and a side of broccoli au gratin. Oh, and will you stop by the Jiffy and buy us two bottles – small bottles – of Naya. Don't get that filtered stuff you got last time."

"Okay… Shana?"

"What?"

I suddenly lost the power of speech.

"What is it, Jamie?" In the background, Mark had started singing "Truckin'" by the Grateful Dead. Very appropriate considering he was the type of third-rate frat boy wannabe who would have stuck a Dead sticker on his parents' hand-me-down Audi as a sign of rebellion and independence.

"I love you. You know that, right?"

She told me that it might be a good idea for me to pick up a couple of videos, so I phoned in the order to Home Cooked and used its preparation time – fifteen to twenty minutes – to go get a couple of New Releases – vaguely artsy films, with mildly quotable recommendations from prominent critics – and scheduled everything like a champ. Right when I walked into Home Cooked my order was ready. I was pleased with myself.

I had to knock on Shana's door three times and wondered if perhaps they had gone out suddenly for some reason (the lights were dimmed in the front room, even though it was cloudy outside, too cloudy to really see anything in Shana's English basement without artificial lighting). On the fourth knock, Mark answered the door, shirtless in a pair of jeans. I studied his smooth, tan chest. He stood with such confidence, so unlike me who had been tested for physical retardation in the Third Grade and had never quite recovered from the trauma. The examining physician's note to my parents read that "the results ultimately were inconclusive." And just then I rediscovered. Compared to Mark, compared to nearly anyone, I was pathetic. I was screwed.

"Hey. Jamie, right?"

"Yeah, what's up?"

We did that firm handshake thing again. This time Mark bested me. I could see that he had a future as an adulterer, an insurance salesman, and a potential child abuser. I had a future of homoerotic fantasies about guys like him, with their firm, control-freak grips. I looked at his eyes, hard and obtuse, the eyes of someone who'd had the exquisite luxury of not wondering what made him so useless, of not having to answer that question as posed by friends and relatives alike. Then I smiled at him, as if to say I was equal to him, just as good as him, just as desirable. He smiled back at me to let me know I was full of shit, that the refutation of my tentative theory had just given him head and swallowed in the other room. Both of us had noses, after all, and both could smell the sex in the air.

Shana came out of her bedroom in a pair of baggy cutoffs and a CompuServe T-shirt. "Hi, Jamie. Just put the food on the table and the videos on the tv in the bedroom. We'll watch them after we eat."

I did as I was told. I listened to their conversation, now in the kitchen, as I stuck the bag of food in the dining area and went into the bedroom. I looked at the bed for evidence – a wet spot, a telltale rumple – but the bed was surgically made, the top blanket's hospital corners staring at me primly. I could smell it though. I could see it happening. I put the new videos next to the ones from the other day that had went unwatched and went to the bathroom to buy some time, to compose myself.

You would've thought that we'd be sitting boy/girl/boy, since Shana was the reason both of us were there and all. But Mark was in the middle. I was stuck on the side, next to the potted plant, yet again peripheral.

No one said much as we took the Styrofoam containers out of the to-go bags. I watched Mark grab Shana's thigh underneath the table, and watched her look back at him with mischief in her eyes, as if she thought they had some private joke that every young couple in the world wasn't in on. As if they were special somehow, even though you could see in her face how her delicate, porcelain features would run weak and pasty and you just knew he'd botch his life up somehow. I tried to change the course of the lunch.

"So, Shana. Can I ask you something?"

"Uh huh."

"Umm, like what…" I was getting tongue-tied again, "what should we, like, do tonight?"

Mark took a bite of his grouper. Shana took a sip of her water. I took my cue, and tore into my French fries with great abandon.

"God, Jamie! Etiquette much?" To save time at meals, I often took a few bites at once. My technique also allowed me to avoid the indelicacy of having, for example, an onion from a hamburger hanging out of my mouth. However, I'm sure I at times looked like a circus seal with a mouthful of fish.

"Sorry, Shana. I'm just really hungry, that's all."

Shana sighed, leaned back in her chair, and stretched out her legs. Her extended calves caressed mine, with no embarrassment or apprehension whatsoever. I imagined what it must feel like to walk on those legs, so feminine and so average all at once. Then she straightened up and took her legs away.

We ended up not doing anything that evening. After we ate, Shana and Mark went and took another shower, and I just sat in front of the tv watching baseball with the mute on and trying to decipher what they were saying. When they finally got out of the shower, they went to their bedroom. I waited for someone to emerge for about forty-five minutes, but all I could hear was a This Mortal Coil album. So I decided to take Matt up on his offer. Even though it was after four, I got a hold of him at Ricky's.

"Women are coozes, Jamie. That's what I keep telling you. Like take Stephanie for example."

I thought about times I could've. That girl was easier than Jello pudding.

"I went through all this shit with Keith, you know, right? And then I told Autrell to call Devin to get Devin to call her and tell her to call me. This was right after I'd called you."

"Yeah... can we stop at the next gas station? I really need to use the bathroom."

Matt looked at me sharply. "Yeah, so, anyway, she didn't call me. So Ricky and I drove up to the Mall..."

"Which one? Crestview?"

"Yeah, and we decided to go in because Ricky needs something from Radio Shack."

"Right." I crossed my legs to avoid potential leakage.

"So, anyway, we go to the entrance by the Chick-Fil-A, and inside the Chick-Fil-A," here Matt paused for dramatic purposes, "right there were Stephanie and William Kenneth."

"That skinhead guy? From the, oh, what is that shit called, the Guardians of the White Cross?"

"Right, Jamie. Exactly." Matt smiled at me beatifically.

"Damn, kid. Steph's such a wigger and all that I thought, no offense, right, that if she was going to step out it would've been with Autrell." I was acting surprised, but the truth was I'm sure she had gone that route as well. Stephanie had already had two abortions, and from all accounts had the sexual history of a small-town burlesque dancer twice her age.

Matt looked at me curiously again. We were perfect friends in that each of us could see how irrevocably damaged the other's love life was, but had very little knowledge of our own. We pulled into the gas station.

"I'll come in with you, Jamie. You want anything to drink?"

"Nah."

I went into the bathroom and stood in front of the urinal. Inside the stall, I could hear kissing and sucking and loud, jagged breathing. My pulse raced, like a heroine in a romance novel that met her soulmate on page ten and had to wait another two hundred pages to be in his arms. I finally managed to relieve myself but took my time zipping up, washing my hands, and combing my hair. In the stall, I heard someone climax.

There was a phone right outside the bathroom door and I decided I would check my messages, to maybe kill some time before they came out of the bathroom. No messages, but I stood there holding the phone ornamentally for a minute or so until they came out. But they had yet to emerge. Chickening out, I walked briskly back to Matt's car, so we could go somewhere and do something.

"Did you drown in there?"

"Yeah."

Matt tried to start his car, but it wouldn't turn over. "Goddamn it."

"Matt, you obviously just flooded the engine. Give it a second."

"That's not what I'm talking about. Jamie, why doesn't she just stand up to them. I'd get a place with her, you know I would."

"I know."

"I love her. Yeah, maybe she's a slut, and I know she doesn't even know what it is to love someone, but I would give her everything."

"Maybe you don't have what she needs. Matt, maybe no one does."

Matt was crying uncontrollably. I put my arm around him, even though the self-proclaimed homeless Vietnam vet begging for money in front of the store was looking at us strangely.

"Matty, think about where she lives and who she lives with. Think about how much like her mom she is, just in different clothes. She's one of those people that, if they didn't have sex drives, they'd be okay. They might solve their problems some other way. You know?" At this point, I was starting to cry a little also. The couple from the bathroom – I just knew it was them – walked out. Two little skaterats, identical short haircuts, except one of them had the faintest etching of breasts. The girl darted her tongue through the aperture of her lips at me several times, lizard-like. I ignored her.

"Let's get out of here, Jamie." His car finally started.

When we got back to his house, Matt decided that he wanted to be by himself for a while, so I left and drove around some. Then I went home. My dad was in his room with the door closed and I turned on the tv, watched some stock car racing, and fell asleep.

I woke up to the phone ringing and the sound of a car exploding as it crashed into a wall.

"Yello?"

All I could hear was sobbing.

"Hello? Who's there?"

I heard some sniffling. I decided to get tough with the caller. I'd had my share of tears that day.

"Look, I'm going to hang up the phone."

"Jamie, I need you…"

"Who is this? Stephanie?"

"Who the hell is *Stephanie*?" From the timbre of the scream, from the utter petulance, I knew who it was.

"Sorry… never mind. What's wrong?"

"I need you to come over. Right now."

"Well, I don't know, Shana. I think I'm busy. My dad and I are going to Wal-Mart or something."

"Forget it!" She hung up the phone.

LACKEY

I pulled up to her front door in my own time without anything in tow, no bags of takeout, no movies, nothing like that. I was determined to stand up to her, to tell her to stop dicking me around.

I walked into Shana's front door and saw her lying on the carpet in a fetal ball. She appeared to be naked except for a blanket wrapped around her breasts and her privates.

"Jesus fucking shit, Shana. What is wrong with you?"

She rolled over and looked at me. She wasn't crying anymore but her left eye had been blackened. She pulled herself to a sitting position and, in a low, serious, uncondescending voice – one I had never heard from her before – said to me, "Jamie, there are a lot of things we need to talk about. Get us some Cokes out of the refrigerator."

I stood over her, noticing flecks of dried blood under her nostril. Her eyes were wide and scared. The house was oppressively hot and smelled like it had been shut up for a week, kind of like when people go on vacation. Unable to control myself, I cracked a smile, thinking of how Mark reeked of English Leather – like some kind of fifty-year old high school geometry teacher or something.

"I'll be right back. Okay?"

I went into Shana's kitchen and grabbed a couple of cokes and a half-empty can of Pringles, thinking back to how many times I had sold out other friends and girlfriends I had to spend a couple of hours with her. How many plans I had changed, how many people I'd stood up. I wondered what it was like, the shock of being hit by him, what the space between the first and second or third punches felt like. Was she surprised? Did she try to block? To hit back? I couldn't ask her. I *wouldn't* ask. I wouldn't sympathize. I put one of the cokes back in the refrigerator, left the chips on the kitchen counter, and as quietly as possible went out the kitchen door, waiting until I was in my car to open the can.

For one reason or another – and there were reasons – leaving Shana crumpled up on the floor seemed like a tangible victory, at least as opposed to driving home crying from her house, listening to Smiths' tapes and eating frosted doughnuts from the Wa Wa store. I turned on the radio and the Will To Power "Baby I Love

Your Way/Freebird" medley came on. I put in on the back speakers and turned the bass up as far as it would go, wanting to fill my car with the synthesized sounds of suburban longing.

I knew exactly where I was driving. Past the Target Greatland and the shining new Fuddrucker's. Past the 24-hour Walmart, taking a right at the Golden Arches. I had made a decision. The air smelled like fresh plastic; clear, strong, and definite.

I had the hardest time remembering where Stephanie lived. It was one of those tract home neighborhoods where every house is pushed in together on tiny parcels of grass, the neighborhoods that poor white trash move to when they want to convince themselves they've moved up to the middle class. I took a right into a culdesac and came across her car. I pulled behind her car and cut the engine, but I was so excited that I inadvertently revved the gas pedal. "Idiot!" I cursed myself.

Very quietly, I walked up to her bedroom window. I could hear some type of therapeutic female pop music playing, something like "oh, oh/ building a mystery/ at Bath and Body Works." I could smell her even from ten feet outside, remembered that time we'd gone to see a concert at this since closed-down local club, and I had pressed my front against her back, the sway of the mosh pit just like us dryfucking, my jeans against her skirt making me hard, making me come. It was better than any sex I'd ever had, because it was so totally anonymous that it all came down to matching parts. I had no idea what she was doing inside the window though. Back then, she didn't know my name, but I'd known hers from the start.

I crept up those last few steps and squatted behind the shrub in front of her window. There really was no risk – she wouldn't notice me unless she was wistfully staring out the window, which I sure as hell knew she wasn't the type to do. I found my vantage point. I keyed in.

She was lying on her floor, face down in a bra and boxer shorts, drawing two women kissing with very bright colored pencils. The women's eyes were sad, but they had a certain – well, shit, they didn't have anything. It was a really crappy drawing made by an ordinary girl on her bedroom's cheap, bristly carpet. Just another girl with a lipstick lesbian fantasy but it made my heart race all the same. I took a sip of my coke. Could Stephanie hear the bubbles popping and fizzing? No she couldn't. She was immersed in the energy of creation. She was making drawings.

And it was enough for me to watch, to know how her stuffed animals were arranged in a row at the head of her bed, to observe how open glossy magazines were strewn all over the floor. I never thought of Stephanie as the type of girl who actually took the beauty tips from *Seventeen* to heart. Somehow, that was comforting to me. I pushed my body close to the wall of her house. Soon she would probably get called to dinner, or she'd have to go into the other room to get her dad a beer or something. I didn't know – it wasn't like I was omniscient. But I knew one thing. I had finally seen Shana broken. I took a gloating, triumphant sip of my soft drink, knowing that one cycle was over while another one was just beginning. Let peace begin with me!

(5) Public Access

I.

The stage awash, as always, in deliquescent blue light. The light of stars - Sinatra and his Rat Pack, Elvis on his comeback tour - artists at the peak of their form. People for whom singing was more than just opening your mouth and letting words come out. People who knew that rocking a live crowd was communion and soulbearing, pleading and just telling. And he is one of those people, a legend in the making an - as yet-undiscovered diamond in the rough. A man with Savile Row style, a one-take crooner with an aquiline nose and sculpted cheekbones that are the essence of refinement, a totemic blend of the cool, composed swingin' single singers of yore and a fiercely modern - yet always romantic - sensibility. Carver Jackson.

(Liner notes for In a Carver Mood, RCA records, 2000)

I'm perfectly aware of course that I couldn't sign my name to those liner notes. Someone else would have to author the words that proved once and for all that I had finally, momentously arrived. But I kept rewriting that script as diligently as I would rehearse my repertoire of Gershwin, Porter, Motown and Brill. I never, ever left making history to chance.

I would always read the latest version of my notes before I'd go to the studio. They affirmed me, letting me know how far I'd come - a year or so ago, I'd gotten that Polygram rep to listen to my tape, and he commented favorably on my timbre upon returning it to me - and he practically said that it might not be too long before I actually hit it big. All I could do is make my opportunities whenever I saw them present themselves; even though I was only doing open mikes and – of course – my show for the time being, I knew very well that at any moment fame could strike me, sweep me up and take me out of Jacksonville and on to what this cornetist I met on AOL called 'the circuit'. It wasn't completely improbable in any case.

On the way to the Continental Cable studio I sang along to a tape I'd made in conjunction with a buddy of mine who had a MIDI setup when I wanted to see how I would sound with an orchestra. I was pretty damned good if I say so myself; on "I get a kick out of you" my voice soared above the synthesized strings and electronic drums and boomed out of the speakers with all the bravura of a Crosby. Debonair, sure, romantic; it was a voice infectious with optimism yet shadowed by the knowledge of not getting a kick out of something, of ennui and disappointment and confusion. I loved my version of the Porter chestnut and would often listen to it over and over again on my way to perform.

I got to the studio right on time and got my electric-blue silk-blend double-breasted number out of the suit bag in the hatchback. We were taping tonight. I needed to look and sound my best; I had every intention of sending this tape to that new BET on Jazz channel, since they seemed to play local people who had polished, professional presentations and good bands backing them. I looked smooth on the screen; over at Computer Pavilion where I've been working for a little bit, people come in and recognize me from the show and compliment me on how good I sounded on the public access. Professional, they would say. Tonight was going to be my night to kick it to the next level though!

Public Access

I came out of the Men's Room in my suit with my hair slicked back and smiled at the receptionist, a jittery, oft-divorced plum who could stand to drop about fifty pounds. We'd had an affair once - more correctly, a disastrous movie date culminating abruptly when she walked out after thwarting my attempt to shove my hand down her pants - but have since been on cooler terms. She didn't return my smile, but all musicians and artists in general know that sexual tension is the province of the creative. So I just let it go. I was on in fifteen anyway.

II.

"I really don't know what's left for you to do, Carver. Three Grammies, multi-platinum status, you've conquered Broadway, the situation comedy. The fragrance line...I have to ask you, Carver, what's next? I'll just ask you what the headline asked on this week's People," here the interviewer pauses to hold the cover up to the camera's eye, "is this the Carver Millennium?"

I shifted into a more comfortable position in my seat, visibly relaxed even under the heat of the CNN Center lights. I had my interview patter down; when you're one of the big boys - i.e. Streisand, Michael Jackson, Sting - the media types clue you in. The producers come out and give you hints on how to present yourself like an éminence grise, like a force to be reckoned with. This was my first time on Larry King Live, but I want to say that his people treated me with the utmost in respect and consideration even from the start. Even while asking tough questions, they conducted themselves with aplomb and remarkable restraint.

"Larry," I started off, plaintively without beseeching him in any significant way, "I come from simple beginnings." Here I took off my glasses and looked into the camera. Larry King was but a conduit; I was speaking to Mr. and Mrs. America. My fans, to whom I gave and gave until I couldn't anymore, then gave some more. "I haven't told this to many people, but my singing comes

comes from a certain, palpable heartache. The heartache that informs blues music, for example."

"Yeah, of course."

"When I decided to interpret Hootie and the Blowfish's 'Let Her Cry', I knew that I had big shoes to fill. The song was obviously deeply personal to Darius and the boys. Let the tears fall down like rain. Yeah. But I thought of the woman when doing my version. Why was she crying? Why were there so many tears, so much sadness in the world for that matter?" I clearly saw Larry King, the most trusted man in American media perhaps ever, take off his glasses and wipe a tear from his eyes. I was speaking from the heart, yes. But Larry and I were true professionals. We knew what made good television. And you could say that one seemingly forgettable interview paved the way for my - if I do say so myself - distinguished career as a telejournalist.

(Carver Country: An Autobiography, Carver Jackson, Random House, 2024)

"Tom, this coffee tastes like piss. It's stale. There are six doughnuts on this table, all with bitemarks in them, and my goddamn band isn't here. Where's Bill? Peter? What the fuck, am I supposed to go a cappella? We've got soundcheck now!

Tom was the cameraman, an all-around good guy whose work wasn't at all hampered by his intermittent alcoholic binges. Bill did my keyboards and programming and Peter was my guitarist. I knew this would happen - Bill and Peter have been freezing me out since we did rehearsal at Pete's and I had a bit too much to drink. I ended up throwing up in his kitchen sink, clogging it beyond where I could unclog it with a handful of paper towels, and leaving without mentioning my indiscretion to either of them. I'd called them a few times since to set up rehearsals, but I'd always gotten their machines and never gotten my calls returned. I started to worry that the rift between us was perhaps not fixable and that they wouldn't be bothered to show up in my hour of need.

PUBLIC ACCESS

Tom wasn't listening to me. He was reading Playboy and sipping on a bottle of non-alcoholic beer. I clapped my hands twice to get his attention, but he didn't so much as twitch, so I walked over to him, grabbed the magazine out of his hands, and ripped it into two down the spine. His jowls puffed out and he looked like he wanted to fight.

"What do you think you're doing, Carver? I was reading that"

"What the hell do you think you're doing? I asked you a question, you sit there and drink goddamn Sharp's. Where's my band?"

"I don't know. Am I your session musicians' keeper? There's a payphone outside - go call them. And you go on in thirty minutes, no matter what. So they're either here or you go Karaoke."

"No, you'll wait as long as I say you'll wait. I'm the artist here, the singer. I'll tell you when to stand up, when to pick up the camcorder, and when to push record. And more close-ups this time. Focus in on me. This has to look as good as possible; I'm dubbing it and sending it to labels. I was a dot in the middle of the screen last week."

"Hey Brenda, this is Carver. Is Bill home?"

I could hear her chomping away on a mid-afternoon snack in the background. Brenda had gained forty pounds in the nine months she and Bill had cohabitated. I kept telling him to just tell her to move her stuff out. She was a really unpleasant, colicky woman whom I could never imagine having any interest in.

"Uh, I think he's working late. I don't know what to tell you. Maybe you should call back." I hung up. Bill was the weak link anyway to start with, and if he couldn't be relied upon, then to hell with him. If Pete hurried down, we could just do it with my voice and his acoustic guitar. The thing that distinguishes my voice from that of the pack, the also-rans and the never-weres, is its versatility. I could belt out a jazz tune but I could also do a sensitive ballad if the situation demanded it. I've never gotten complaints for my singing at wedding receptions, for example.

I didn't have my address book with me. I could only guess at Pete's number, and since I had one quarter left, it had to be a pretty damned good guess. I knew the first three digits were 766.

But was it 9732 or 9237? 9327? I dropped the quarter into the slot and punched the buttons, feeling like some weird sort of itinerant small-stakes gambler who had failed in Vegas and was getting ready to admit defeat in Atlantic City. The phone rang three times, three of those ponderously choleric analog rings that characterize rural, nowhere neighborhoods and backwards clumps of people. Right before the fourth ring, someone finally picked up.

"Paxon A.M.E. - can I help you," an elderly black man asked, someone who was distinctly not Pete. For example, Pete was white enough to enjoy Canadian pop music - stuff like Barenaked Ladies and The Crash Test Dummies. He was young besides. Did I have the right number?

"Uh, yes. Sir, I'm looking for 766-9732. Is this it?"

"Ah, no! You've reached Seven Six Five…" I hung up. The dialogue was over.

"Lydia, hey!" Lydia swiveled toward me in the chair, sharply resembling a human incarnation of Garfield the Cat. "Can you do me a solid?"

"What is it?" She squinted at me suspiciously, like a mother checking her child's head for lice. Things would've been different if I'd at least called her to apologize, maybe.

"Well, I'm sorta out of quarters," I said, chuckling, "and I need to round up my boys. I have to go on in twenty minutes." I went over and sat on the edge of her desk to make things seem more intimate. "Maybe I can use your phone?"

"Switchboard's closed. Sorry. No can do." She went back to the quiz in her Glamour magazine, 'Does Your Man Hate Women?'. She would not be moved.

I had to see if Tom could be persuaded to help me out.

III.

CJ: In a real sense, asking me what sex is is like asking me to define jazz or air. Jazz is my lifeblood and I've brought it to the masses. It's a rare privilege to be able to share my gift with so many millions. And I don't have to tell you about air. But sex to me is kind of meaningless without love attached to it.

Having the profile I have, there is naturally a certain type of woman who will always find her way backstage, who will find out what hotel you're at. I've grown accustomed to that, although I think it distracts me from other things. So often these women just want to sleep with your mystique.

RS: Right...

*CJ: At this point, I want a soulful love (*Editor's Note: Jackson's 'Soulful Love' single is number one on the Pan-European charts as we go to press), *one I can feel inside of me. I want a soulmate, I don't think that's too much to ask.*

Are you familiar with the Kama Sutra?

("Carver Jackson: He's Got Jazz, He's Got Soul, and He Wants More", Rolling Stone; March 3, 2004)

"Now, tell me Tom. How the hell are we going to have me singing into a karaoke machine and not make me look like a complete idiot?"

Tom smiled benignly, draining his bottle for dramatic effect. "Carver, I've thought all this through. In the storeroom we have a machine, one of those ninety-nine dollar ones they sell at Target. It's about yea high," he said, pointing at the middle of his thigh.

"That could work," I conceded.

"You wanted close-ups anyway. You'll get tight face shots for the most part, nothing below your waist. You'll be like Elvis on Ed Sullivan!"

Elvis! I didn't buy it for a minute. But what else could I do? We had about ten minutes until the live transmission of my show. Enough time, as it turned out, to dig out the machine and clip a microphone to the left hand speaker because the Karok2000 didn't even have input-output jacks. I picked up a napkin from out of the doughnut box and began dabbing at my upper lip and my forehead - trying to appear dry, working to seem composed.

"Hey, Tommy! What tapes you got in there?" I was starting to warm up to the concept somewhat. If my voice was good, it would rise above the technical difficulties and the musician no-shows. I could still rock the mike. I could still emanate charisma as I'd done before. I was still Carver Jackson!

"Uh, all I could find was… Mariah Carey." Tom and I weren't friends, but he sounded profoundly embarrassed for me. "The backing vocals will be there, and I'll put in the video that came with the tape on Monitor #2 so you can follow along with the lyrics."

"Goddamnit, Tom. How long is this tape?"

"Twenty-seven minutes and forty seconds. Enough time to get in and out. I'll give you the cue to hit play on the machine in about 2 minutes right before I start fading your theme out."

"You mean I can't even talk to the people? Say 'Hello, I'm Carver Jackson, and you can watch my career implode before your very eyes'? This is so-"

Tom looked at me as if completely disgusted. "Career. You're a stockboy at a computer store. Your band stood you up. Get over it…"

The silence hung, malignant and lethal. Eighty seconds to air. I decided to make peace.

"At least tell me which of Mariah's songs I'll be singing."

Tom breathed deeply. "'I'll Be There', 'One Sweet Day', 'Love Takes Time', 'I Don't Wanna Cry', 'Without You', and 'Can't Let Go'."

"That's all? Thank God. I don't have the range for 'Emotions'."

Tom reckoned that the machine had to be turned up as loud as it could go. It was up, way up, so loud that I could hear the upper-register stuff like the strings and the backing harmonies being mangled by distortion. I felt like the Jimi Hendrix of easy-listening soul. Nonetheless, I plugged on. Turgid ballads segued into derivative cover versions, and I kept at it. It's what a performer does, after all.

After my set was over, Tom pushed me out of the door as quickly as possible. He said he had an AA meeting to get to, that he'd been feeling a relapse coming on. Who was I to argue? Midway through my performance, I felt like getting drunk myself.

IV.

Two letters came in the mail that day:

Dear Mr. Jackson,

It is with great regret that we announce the cancellation of your "Carver Jackson Sings Jazz" program. Rest assured that our concerns weren't content-related, but instead are budgetary. Continental Cablevision strives to represent the interests of all of its subscribers as well as the community at large, and we feel that what is essentially a showcase for your not inconsiderable talents attracts only a niche audience.

If you have any questions regarding your cancellation, please call Misty James during normal business hours Monday through Friday at 731-7755. She would be happy to discuss further the details of our programming changes.

Sincerely,

Kelly Wallace

Dear <u>Carver Jackson,</u>

Congratulations! You have been selected as the January 1996 Computer Pavilion Employee of the Month for Store 097 in Jacksonville, FL. Your <u>diligence,</u> <u>attention to detail</u> , and your <u>exceptional work ethic</u> have made you a source of pride in your home store as well as here in corporate headquarters. We're proud to have you aboard!

Now we believe that exceptional, beyond-the-call-of-duty performance deserves rewards! Our reward schedule is tripartite - that is, it has three phases.

Right now you're in Phase One. You've received your confirmation letter (as evidenced by the fact that you are reading it right now!). You don't have to do anything yet but wait for Phase Two to begin!

Phase Two will begin in two to three weeks. In this phase, you will reap the rewards of your accomplishments! Via UPS, you will be receiving a handsome 8x10 'Employee of the Month' plaque with your name inscribed just below the caption! This phase is also marked by the beginning of your Preferred Parking Privileges (PPP) on February 1. Your PPP will be in effect for the entire month of February, so enjoy it!

Phase Three isn't a phase as cut and dry as the first two - it lasts all year long! You and all the other Employees of the Month nationwide will have your names automatically entered into a sweepstakes drawing with the winner to receive...

An All Expense Paid Trip For Two To Hawaii!

So keep your fingers crossed, Carver Jackson, and recognize that hard work reaps its rewards! Congratulations again! Hopefully we'll see YOU on the sands!

Sincerely,

Ruskin Boutwell III,

VP in charge of Employee Liaisons

I could've done a number of things at this point. Gotten in my car and driven, gone to see my ex-girlfriend Mindy who got knocked up by a Navy guy on his way out of town. Now she lives at Jacksonville Beach and sells dope to the surfers and the kids from Fletcher High School and takes care of her kid. I thought about going over to Bill's or Pete's, calling them out and beating the hell out of them until the cops came. But I decided none of those options were consistent with my new Employee Of The

Month standing. So instead I went inside and watched the video, mostly to get it over with.

What wasn't a mess about it? Tom must have had two hundred watts aimed at my face – I looked like a P.O.W. being questioned about troop movements. Perhaps not entirely on purpose, he panned the camera down, showing the karaoke machine quite clearly in a number of shots, even once zooming in on the taped-on microphone.

Worst of all though were the vocals themselves. As I sat there watching my Cable TV farewell, I couldn't hear my voice at all. Tom, the soundman, apparently didn't expect the Karok2000 to have a false sense of stereophonic sound. For thirty minutes, all I could hear were the saccharin MIDI strings and the android backing singers garbled by the excessive volume. All of it mashed and blended into an anonymous wall of sound.

(6) Getting By

I was doing my job when I saw them. Standing at the corner of Wisconsin and Nebraska on the side of the street with the Payless and the plasma clinic, trying not to let on that I was uncomfortable in any way even though I only had a windbreaker on and it was an early January Tuesday in Washington. I was selling mock-ups of designer perfumes and colognes. You know. If you like Polo, you might be able to tolerate Water Polo if you have no sense of smell whatsoever.

And I had a technique developed, as all salesmen did. A heavyset guy comes up and I'd smile at him like I pitched and he caught on the same high school team. "Hey, Big Guy! What kind of cologne do you wear," I'd ask him, an unchangingly engaging smile on my face the whole time. Sometimes he'd buy my crap, sometimes he wouldn't. The trick to success was attention to detail. Desensitization to process, to self-effacement. That was how I dealt with men.

Women required something different. Even if they were sixty years old or had dandruff all over their shoulders, you had to make yourself flirt with them. But I knew how to flirt meaninglessly with the best of them - boosting my mother's ego over the phone after the divorce taught me that. With tired middle-aged women, I would front like they were alluring and worldly and still beautiful even after all these years. I never let on who they really were during my sales pitch. If they were ever to find out that they were these non-descript big-assed women in unflattering overcoats, I wasn't going to be the one to tell them. I had a quota. Cologne sold itself when I sold myself.

But of course the customers I'm about to tell you about were neither heavyset men nor middle-aged women.

Ever since I was granted my discharge, I hadn't really been bothered by destructive thoughts so much. I don't want to bore you or anything with talking about the treatments, but they really do help you to cope. They help you see what's what, really, and give you an idea of how you can be a better person, how you can make a difference. So I stopped thinking about sex all the time like I used to before going to Kingsland, instead focusing my energies on getting a job and getting by. Learning not to take life so seriously, to be sociable. Following the advice on the "One Day At A Time" and "Footprints" plaques my grandmother sent me after my first suicide attempt. Stuff like that.

In any case, I wasn't the ugliest guy in the world either. A lot of women go for my type - short, skinny, almost studious or intellectual. A couple of girls even have asked me if I'm an artist or a poet during our conversations on my corner. I try to cultivate that image -- sometimes I would even wear these glasses I found at the flea market down in Georgetown with clear lenses in them to create the impression that I wouldn't be selling cologne forever, to make the customers think I could be doing something better with my life. And sometimes that little trick made all the difference between a sale and a customer just passing by. But all of this is irrelevant; I wasn't even wearing my glasses on the day I met Emily and Natasha.

The street had been deserted for a few minutes when I saw this fat girl in a safety orange bubble jacket come out of the plasma clinic. She had a pretty face, but was large boned. You know what I mean; the girl was unbelievably big. Like if you were on a date with her and your car stalled out, you'd make her help push -- that kind of big. But she was dressed right and smiled at me, so I smiled back.

She had been staring at me for a couple of minutes and I was thinking of just leaving; the sky was starting to cloud up and my father wanted me to hit Safeway for some Hot Pockets on my way home. Right before I left, she started talking to me though. "What's in your box?"

"Stuff. You know, cologne. I'm selling cologne." I was starting to sweat, even in the cold. My legs and back started to itch all at once, like they wanted to grow hair or something. Conversations like this were what always got me in trouble to start with, you know?

"Cologne, huh?" Just then the door to the plasma clinic opens and the most beautiful girl I had ever seen in my life walked out. She couldn't have been more than five foot tall, ninety pounds. Her teeth were polished and flossed, immaculate; her hair beyond criticism in a cherry-red bob cut. She was like something out of a JC Penney circular, slim and elegant in form-fitting, tapered-ankled jeans and a tasteful, olive drab henley sweater. Her eyes were the deep iridescent azure of dime store nail polish. The girl was a perfect fit, the ideal blend of the sublime and the average; the approachable girl you'd never approach but instead would watch defy gravity and float skyward, free of ballast or earthly attachment. I could feel my sex drive coming back, almost as those lapses before had never happened.

The girl of my dreams walked behind the other girl and covered her eyes with her hands. Loud enough to be heard over the passing cars and the blustering wind, she announced, "I had to use the bathroom!"

"I hope you washed afterwards," her friend replied, plucking her friend's hands off of her face. My stomach felt like I had just driven fast over railroad tracks; this beautiful girl could rub grape jam all over my face and I'd be turned on, distracted to where I couldn't stand it. It was like Doctor Friedan said, I guess. I have a rampant libido. And that was something I couldn't let myself think about. I unbuttoned my jacket, let the cold wind tear through my t-shirt as I stared into my box and waited for these girls to walk away.

Their voices died as they finally departed and as I looked up the fat girl in the Michelin man bubble jacket looked back at me even as her friend's arm straddled her lower back. Was she mouthing a goodbye? I pretended not to notice. I became very conscious of my movements, convinced that my right foot was noticeably heavier than my left. It was sticking to the sidewalk. Of course, it was gum. It was that kind of encounter in that kind of day.

I was still scraping my foot against the curb when the girls walked back in my direction. The beautiful girl was out in front, as if the litter-strewn Wisconsin Avenue sidewalk were her own personal runway. She was popping this blue gum in her mouth really sexily, blowing bubbles I could see from down the block. A couple of homeless men fresh out of the plasma clinic were standing there checking her out, even while knowing they had never had a shot at a girl like this except in a dark alley. Her friend was in tow, lagging behind; they walked towards me hand in glove.

"Hey! " she shouted at me loud enough to make a reluctant buyer turn around to see if she was talking to him. "You have a girlfriend?"

"Uhhh, no!" My voice cracked high and girlish, like it always did when I let my guard down. "Why do you want to know?"

"I was wondering if you want to go on a date." The fat girl was in the background, staring blankly like an extra in an action movie. I was stunned into silence. "Hurry up and tell me, I haven't got all day."

" First you have to tell me your name." I felt myself beginning to hyperventilate.

"I'm Natasha. And this is my friend Emily." Natasha gestured behind her towards Emily, who stood there as unanimated as a worn-out icebox being auctioned off.

"Yeah, Hi. I'm Darrell." Natasha was sizing up my outgrown windbreaker, my frayed cords, my stiff, flouride-white tennis shoes. I was just standing there letting her watch me, wiggling my toes inside my shoes and feeling the dirt and grime inside my socks.

Neither of the girls even cracked a smile. Natasha finally spoke up. "So where are you going to take her?"

I felt my eyes begin to glaze over. I stared at a hangnail on Emily's hand, imagined yanking at it with my teeth, unraveling her skin and her lard and her muscle, stripping her to ivory bones. She could be beautiful, I reckoned. I used Natasha's pen to write down Emily's number, settling for second best.

Getting By

"Now, Dare. You know these conversations have been a bit one-sided lately, almost as if you're scared to open up with me. You do trust me, don't you?"

"Yeah, Dad, I trust you a lot. I thought you knew that." He smiled at me cagily and I smiled back. We were like a bad marriage. He was the melodrama-ridden wife who waited up with a rolling pin and a laundry list of guilt trips; I was the tomcat husband, running around all the time, getting what I could where I could. And despite my infidelities, I usually found time to replace the bandages on the cysts on his back

We sat at opposite ends of the couch with a sports memorabilia show on QVC flashing mutely on the tv in front of us. Mom left right after I graduated from high school, leaving behind a note that took three pages to say "I kept it together for the kid and I was too chicken shit to leave". I never really thought of her that much when she lived at home anyway; we weren't the kind of family that went to movies or football games or museums. Instead we videotaped network sitcoms, read self-help books from the supermarket, or exercised on mail-order body part isolator machines.

And when she left there was a certain indefinite hope. The summer she went solo my dad became a total badass, coming home drunk and throwing vases, getting arrested for fights at sports bars (he's a lifelong Yankees fan living an hour's drive from Baltimore), and - for the first time in years - acting like a man. Cyrus Carpenter, a lifelong civil servant, was dangerous. He lost weight, got a tan, and began sleeping with worn-out cocktail waitresses. He let down his guard, never buttoning his shirt very far up, flashing a gold necklace amidst the wrinkles and the gray chest hairs.

And then he settled down and waited to die. My father became a captive to his second mortgage, to beer steins over the fireplace and to wood-paneled walls. He had to know how he looked to me, 150 pounds overweight in a tattered brown terry cloth robe, not exactly a role model for troubled youth. He had to want me to escape his fate; his birth certificate and his DNA code were nothing short of promissory suicide notes. So I looked into his eyes and decided to just tell him. To tell him that I was going to take a chance on living again, that I was going to go to the next level. Much like Bill Laimbeer hawking autographs on cable, I was going to make the best out of my circumstances. My dad was damned to losing his glasses as they sat atop his forehead and to pissing in his Lazyboy; Emily - maybe - would rescue me. Would justify my love.

Before I could go into my pitch though, he started talking. "Son, I need you to do something for me." His eyes were bright, full of trust.

"What is it, dad?"

"I need you to make me some lunch."

"Like what," I asked, stiffening. "We have some tuna and chicken up in the cupboard. You want chicken salad?"

"No, I want something a bit *heartier*. Make some Hamburger Helper. Not that three cheese kind though, make cheeseburger macaroni." He was getting so old so quickly. I'd learned too little from him, and wondered how many Saturday afternoons we'd spend like this before it got worse. Would I get out before senility washed over him like a blood tide? Would he really miss me if I just one day up and left? It had taken him so long even to be able to look me in the face after he picked me up from the hospital.

"All right, Dad. Whatever you want . . . " I went into the kitchen and started browning some ground beef. It was the cheap kind he always bought when he did the shopping. Every time he went to the Safeway, we ate garbage for a week -- ice milk and Shasta and store brand chips. I lidded the pan as the meat sizzled underneath and returned to the living room where he was going to hear me out, goddamnit.

"Dad . . . I have something to tell you. I think I'm -"

"Would you mind doing something else for me? I need you to get my heating pad off of my bed."

"All right. Anything else? Something to drink, maybe," I asked, with a slight edge on my voice.

"Yeah, just grab that jug of tea from inside the refrigerator and hand it to me. Before you get the heating pad," he instructed. My father had pulled his nail file from inside the remote control pocket on his recliner chair, and had started to saw at the calluses on his feet. Delicate particles of dust wafted from the sole of his foot; this Saturday afternoon that only promised televised bowling was getting to be too much to bear. I stomped to my room and grabbed my wallet and a flannel shirt. I had to get away from that house as quickly and uneventfully as possible.

I avoided the kitchen and the family room, taking the exit through the living room my mother had occupied before her departure. "Dad, I'm leaving - the meat's still on the stove," I called out.

As I was closing the door, I heard his response, a second or two too late for me to turn around. What was it you wanted to talk to me about, he asked. He knew I wanted something all along. He had just waited way too long to find out what it was.

I wasn't driving around for too long before I reached into my wallet for Emily's number. The sun was pale and granular, just beginning to set behind the upscale cheerlessness of Bethesda and the working-class, chain restaurant desolation of Rockville. I drove around through most of Pretty Hate Machine looking for one of those curbside phone booths you could use while sitting in your car. I couldn't find any, so I settled for a working phone outside a 7-Eleven, ignoring a homeless guy who kept bugging me for a quarter so he could get on the Internet. I put my finger in my ear and dialed her number.

"Hi . . . is Emily there?"

"This is -"

"Hey, this is Darrel . . . from the other day. The cologne guy, you remember?"

"Hey! How are you?"

"Bored, mostly. I was wanting to see what you were doing tonight. If you wanted to get together maybe, we can go see a movie over at the Uptown. Or we could go to Georgetown and get something to eat wherever you want to go. I have a City Paper if you want me to take a look and see if someone's playing down at the 9:30. Whatever you want-"

"Oh, I really would like to. But Natasha just called me like ten minutes ago or something. So I have to do something with her."

"Darrel, are you still there?" Apparently there had been a silence, a lagtime in which I should have responded but somehow not managed to. There have always been times when I would just black out, just to get by.

"Oh, yeah! I was just thinking about something." My counselor told me I should sound enthusiastic when I talked to women. But not too enthusiastic, he warned me. The trick was keeping myself under control, maintaining my center. Every new experience was a clean slate. Every new person was a second chance.

"Yeah? What were you thinking about?" She really wanted to know. Her voice was all bright and cheerful, reassuring. The voice of someone that wanted to be in love, of someone who wanted to be fun and well-liked by men, by me perhaps. And yet she was not one of the beautiful, untouchable ones, the ones I needed to redeem me. I was getting a stomachache.

"Nothing. It doesn't matter. I have to go."

"Oh, well, call me next week. We'll get together."

"We'll see. I don't know if I'm going to have time." I hung up the phone and went into the convenience store to buy a bottle of Ny-Quil. I knew exactly what I was going to do: go home, make nice with my dad, down the cough syrup, draw the shades, and lie in bed until my father went to sleep. It was something I had done many times before.

Desire. When something is denied you, even for the most logical reasons, you chase it harder and harder until you catch it, until you finally crush the impulse. I psyched myself up for calling Emily Monday afternoon by watching a People's Court marathon on Fox 30 while downing a series of my pop's canned Slimfast shakes. After drinking most of the six-pack and becoming violently ill in the kitchen sink, I was ready to make that call. Not as a means of getting to Natasha, surprisingly enough that wasn't my motive anymore, or at least I didn't think it was. As I dialed Emily's number, I wondered what my motive was exactly.

Emily's phone rang three, almost four times, before some woman answered. "Hello," barked out in a voice forever tainted by Viceroys before breakfast and Sanka before bed. The voice of a weight problem and a leaky roof, of lung cancer and stomach-stapling and nicotine patches. The voice, presumably, of Emily's mother.

Getting By

"Hey there little lady, is Emily home?"

"Son, you need to stop calling here. I told you already three times today-"

"*I* haven't called today. I resent the implication, as a matter of fact - stop wasting my time here, is she home or not?" I asked, feeling my neck start to seize up, my impatience growing. I seriously doubted any male had called Emily at any point in the preceding twelve months. She wasn't a pretty girl, just one I could close my eyes and screw while we both waited for something better to happen along. The kind you'd see on Jenny Jones once she finally topped 300 pounds declaring her love for a death row inmate.

"This is her mother. She's out of town for the weekend. Do you want to give me a message?" I could hear Headline News blasting away in the background as she tapped a virgin cigarette against a table. I loosened my belt. "Son! Yes or no? Do you have a message for me?"

" Stupid bitch… fuck off, die."

Emily star 69'd me ten minutes later.

"Your mother's got some problems."

"Oh, if its not one antidepressant, its another."

"Oh. Sure!" I laughed quickly, then she joined me in good natured laughter. I could hear her mother on the other end, talking alarmingly loud about OJ Simpson, the Pope, and a naked woman with a poodle under her arm. "Who's your mother talking to?"

" Uh, well, you know. Nobody. She's got - you know - problems," Emily added quickly. "Like you said, you know?"

"Not really. My family's pretty normal . . . " I wasn't too into this conversation, occupied as I was with playing solitaire with a deck of my dad's 'Three Slut Night Playing Cards' $_{(TM)}$. I sighed into the phone, letting Emily know she was losing me.

"Never fucking mind. I'm sorry I brought it up," she said, as if to cut me off. The impudence - I couldn't concentrate on solitaire at all! I knew how to play Emily though; I let her sit there and be all pissed off for a minute or so. She was in no position to hang up.

" All right. I'm fine, forget it. So do you still want to go out?" The fire in her voice was gone. I had won.

Getting By

Before I was the last to realize my limitations, I always wondered who it was that dated the ugly. Who wined and dined those with crippled up legs? Who saw that the acne ridden always felt loved? When I was young, the fat, the ugly, the malformed would haunt me, each and every one of them asking more of me than I could deliver *just because they existed*! But I had matured. I had lived through the disappointments of unattended proms. I had suffered silently in mass transit, sitting behind giddy young couples who looked like they would sooner die than unfurl their limbs from each other's fevered grips. I had brooded and bit my tongue, with all the effect of watering dead houseplants. I wanted to be a breeder, to have a piece of the breeders' action. I wanted abortion clinics and sex in Motel 6's and wifeswapping like people used to have before AIDS. Frizzy permed girls on me two at a time in sequined spandex bodysuits.

But these things weren't possible and Emily was. And that was enough. We arranged to meet over in Dupont Circle at one of five convenient Starbucks the next day. The movie, the date could finally happen. It had been way too long since I had been with someone who actually wanted to be with me. Sure, I'd been known to pick up the occasional eighth or ninth grader, buy some cheap, sweet wine, and go at it in the back of my car. But this thing with Emily was different. It had potential to be filled to the brim with lovers' secrets and engagement announcements and shared fantasies of three way sex with Rite-Aid checkout clerks.

All we are is all we are. And everything was falling in place.

Ice pellets were falling from the sky as I approached Starbucks, and I was more than surprised to see Emily and Natasha huddled together under the awning. The moment was laden with soap opera tension; I saw a certain honor in settling for Emily, attempting to venerate the prospects of tepid sex and half-hearted avowals of passion, to liquefy mediocrity and hold it over my head in a jewel-encrusted chalice. But how could I even think of that when Natasha was right there next to her playing Diana Ross to Emily's Florence Ballard? The night was a wire; I stared at Natasha even from twenty feet away and all I could see was her naked, prostrate form. I had a flash of us going at it on the floor of a boys' locker room, me sucking hickeys into her neck while neither of us could escape that terrible dankness and the vitiated smell of industrial-strength disinfectant. I was in love. And she was in love also, that's why she came.

I suppose it was instinct that made me embrace Natasha first. She was all foundation makeup and fake nails and CK1, and I could feel her firmness even through her coat. The kind of girl who ran or did her aerobics every day. I lunged to kiss her on her cheek and she turned her lips in my direction, even while her best friend stood two feet away. It was a brief kiss, but long enough for Emily to go to the counter and get ready to order. I knew this move well; rejection had often pushed me into unblinking practicality, so much easier than thinking about what your body was crying out for at that point. Tousling my hair, Natasha told me she had to go to the bathroom. Be right back. (I hope you wash up afterwards . . .)

I played Emily exactly like I had been taught to by, well, some other girls. "Hey, get me a large Mocha frappe, and I'll see about getting us some seats." I made sure to touch the back of her neck, but I couldn't linger; I saw a few seats at the end of the counter against the window, and knew I had to make my move. The music was piercingly loud: the darkness has a hunger that's insatiable, and the lightness has a call that's hard to hear.

One man sat at the end of the counter with three empty seats to his side. He was a typical DC lawyer or lobbyist, a well-tailored suit, a scarf, an overcoat - the colors all muted and coordinated. And he had that aloof, I'm Snubbing The Homeless expression on his face. He was someone I didn't particularly want to sit by, but they were the only open seats in the place.

Just as I was straddling my jacket over the chairs though, he gestures at me. A wide, sweeping, Charlton Heston parting the Red Sea gesture. He can't even be bothered to say anything to me, just waved his arms as if to say *Be Gone With You. You can't sit here.* I breathed deeply, the acrid stench of my schizophrenia clashing with his sugary, effete cologne. I knew this feeling from high school lunch rooms, from Top 40 dance clubs where I'd try my damnedest to get with fat-assed bleached blonds in acid-washed jeans only to be shot down.

I totally snapped on him. I moved really close - only six inches separated our faces - and laid into him, "Fuck you, little man", I screamed, "Like you can't be bothered telling me the seats are saved. What are you, some kind of deaf mute? Piss off!" I was electrified by the moment. I felt whole. I felt like dancing around Starbucks and doing Indian war whoops. So what if we didn't have a place to sit - I had my self-respect. I walked up to Emily and started prattling away.

"God, you should have seen this asshole over there trying to save the whole fucking counter for his friends. The bitch couldn't even be bothered to say anything. Oh no, not him. He just points at the seats!"

Emily nodded, smiling therapeutically. "The thing was, he couldn't be bothered to say anything, you know? So I just went off on his ass, and I like asked him, you know, 'What are you, some kind of deaf-mute?'" I laughed; I think she smiled again, the imperfect girl trying to be the perfect date. I would put out for her. I would give her my most sacred gift.

"Where is he?"

"He's right over . . . there." I squinted; I think I was beginning to actually need real glasses. We both looked over there only to see him and three other people signing like mad to each other. Emily turned very pale at first, then went crimson - all in the matter of seconds. A little too loud for my taste, she called out, "Fuck you, fuck Natasha, fuck each other, to hell with all this. I'm out." Before stomping out the door, she dumped a venti Mocha frappucino down my shirt.

So I figured that pretty much capped the evening. Emily had disappeared into sidewalk traffic. I was standing in the middle of a coffee bar feeling the collective remonstration of coffee bar patrons. I watched Natasha walk out of the bathroom into the aftermath as if on infrared film, all blotchy and vividly slow-motion. If I had scripted it, she'd have walked by me, leaving me to a rightful lynching by the assembled hearing-impaired coffee lovers. As it was though, she grabbed my hand and whispered "let's go" in my ear through a mist of Watermelon Bubblicious.

Getting By

Roy Rogers, Cineplex Odeon, CVS. We were running at breakneck speed down the dimly-lit Connecticut Avenue sidewalk, past the homeless men holding styrofoam cups on the steps of 9 to 5 businesses, through herds of university students talking too fast and walking too slow. Our love was the love of three minute skating rink pop songs; we were invincible, we had a limited lifetime warranty. We were T-Fal.

Natasha cornered me against the door of my Honda Civic driving my back flush against the door handle, and shoved her tongue down my throat when I noticed something. Kissing her was the taste of bubble gum and vomit; in that first, most prolonged French kiss, I learned the secret of her thinness, I discovered the corrosion that lied just beneath the flawless exterior. The corrosion I knew very well, the corrosion Emily stomped away from as quickly as she could.

She had all the sex appeal of corn chips to me at this point, but I couldn't let her down. The seductive embrace by way of greeting, the running down Connecticut Avenue like purse thieves weren't things that could be neglected; instead, they created an obligation I had to live up to, not one I could shirk like those 10 cd's for One Penny offers I always filled out under assumed names.

The show had to go on, and I am nothing if not a showman. I opened up her door first. We were going for a ride.

I wasn't sure what I wanted to do now that I finally had her alone. I felt that we were too close physically to each other; what had seemed to be an attractive compactness just minutes before suddenly struck me as an unbecoming dwarfishness. I had a phase at Kingsland where I would hide away with a dictionary and just read; I got to the H's before release, quite a ways past dwarf. Every time I looked at her I thought of a secondary definition of dwarf that I had memorized - "a small being, misshapen and ugly and usually skilled as an artificer". I bit my tongue, yet couldn't help but wonder if Natasha was a skilled ceramicist or potter.

Thoughts like that aren't conducive to romance most of the time. I felt like the heroine tied to the railroad tracks in a Dudley Do-right cartoon - I had to do something! I had to end this thing right then and there. I couldn't stand the sight of her. I looked at her and saw druids and circus midgets. I grabbed at her hand and pressed it down on my fly. "Come on, baby. Get me off," I instructed. Get me off. The very thought of my penis has catalyzed hundreds of restraining orders, so I figured it would work its inimitable magic once again.

Not this time and not this girl though. Deliberately, Natasha started stroking me. I was starting to get into it, running red lights and looking for a side street to turn on to. Natasha had the handjob technique common to all neighborhood sluts, the girls with no outward self-esteem who learned every nerve bundle of what it was they were manipulating, who made themselves beautiful, hoping for a big payoff, but getting instead a job in the retail sector and a brood of unwanted, uninspired offspring. I took a right, took a left, weaved my way into the labyrinth of Glover Park's rowhouses and faceless apartment buildings and waited to hear her tell me to stop the car. Pull the fucking car over.

We found a secluded place, got in the back seat, and took our clothes off (we were butt-naked except for our socks). On top of her, I could see her reflection in the hatchback window; as we rocked the car hard enough to make the cologne bottles in the floorboard shake, her eyes had that unmistakable look of someone waiting for something far better than what she had at that moment. Trying and failing to make her come, I couldn't shake the thought that I wouldn't end up calling her. I would never see her again.

(7) Double Play

My intention was not to pick up the 6-4-3, or any of that. Or even to go unassisted. You hope for double plays; you don't plan on them or expect them, as that's hubris, really.

I ran across Michelle during the last frames of an already booze-soaked evening. At a local convenience store, where the lights glared harshly off of goldenrod walls, and the harridans behind the protective glass of the counter squawked unhappily due to hardness of hearing coupled with the loudness of the portable radio, which sang beyond the limitations of its plastic, built-to-break walls.

Not that I knew Michelle's name. I'd seen her, in that way that men like me often see women like her. They hand us our change and we stare at them, awestricken, considering what it must be like to have pink hair or piercings all over our faces. We consider the protrusions of our abdomens, each in turn, and realize that these chicks don't go for men who sort of know wine and how to color-coordinate clothes from the J.Crew catalogue. These chicks want transgression; punk kids in leather pants and dirty t-shirts. These chicks don't want the straight world, the straight life that we represent. So it goes.

I had learned to lower my expectations some time ago. Some men, after all, aren't macks. Aren't players. At twenty-six or thirty, we pay for massages ("ethical inquiries only") and try to keep our hands off the therapist as she works over our hairy, flabby torsos and limbs. We try not to come when we roll over under the sheet. We try not to hold our smiles too long when walking into the woman's office space. I'm the target market for sports talk radio and strip clubs, and that doesn't surprise or upset me.

Still, it was something when I smiled at her and she wrapped her arms around me. Something to smell her; an unmistakable pungency with a floral undercurrent.

Michelle and I released each other, and I got to use the line that always worked for me with other girls: drinks, on my balcony; why don't you come? We bought some girly drinks – Cider, Hard Lemonade – and then deposited her bicycle into the trunk of my late-model American compact.

I carried her mountain bike up the stairs and let her carry the bottles. We passed my scarecrow of a neighbor, who scowled at us on her way downstairs, Hefty Bag in tow. "Another late night," she hissed menopausally, mindful of times when I'd entertained young ladies well into the wee hours.

"Piss off," I replied under my breath. To Michelle, I added, "we don't get along."

"Yeah, me and Samantha pissed off our neighbors a lot too. They called the cops on us and once we got arrested for domestic violence."

"I see," I declaimed while unlocking the door. "Damn."

I rolled the bicycle through the doorway and propped it against the wall. Michelle had launched herself into yet another story about Samantha; her recent ex-girlfriend who Michelle had dumped but wasn't quite over. This one involved Michelle sleeping with Samantha's ex-boyfriend. Though Michelle wasn't attracted to men, really, she "slept with him because he was so nice."

What was there to say to that? "True," I said in a sanitized ghetto manner reminiscent of Budweiser commercials. "Word," I added with an ironic twist to my voice.

I waited for a beat to see if this chick would get my sarcasm. Like I've said, I'm not an attractive man. I have hair on my back and I'm only getting hairier. There's a Cro-Magnon set to my forehead and I boast a ponderous, geologically influenced jawline. So it goes. By the time you've reached the final act of your twenties, you learn to compensate for inadequacies. I could never be an androgyne, but damned if I couldn't skewer and mock pop culture. Damned if I couldn't turn everything into a self-referential exercise in constructing the illusion of my own superiority. Damned if I couldn't flatter whoever I was trying to get with by letting her feel like the only person in the world tuned in to my inside joke.

But not this one. She was immune to my charms, in this respect, at least for right now. So I went to Plan B. "You want to get some weed?" A question asked as I rifled through the new entries on my caller ID; callbacks for jobs I wasn't interested in, cold calls from hot-blooded go-getter phone solicitors, chicks I once chilled with seeking succor and hookups. The usual; I deleted.

"I have some in my bag. You got papers? I lost my pipe."

I smiled and provided a pack of 1.5s. Weed was always a good thing.

Though while she rolled the joint (one of considerable size, thankfully) she continued to vent about this Samantha character, once she'd finished rolling and lit up she mercifully shut up about the whole business. We sat out on the balcony with hard lemonades, alternating tokes with each other while being serenaded by the whir of the ghetto bird above, searchlighting for fugitives or something.

"I love having a balcony. It makes me feel so removed from things on the street," I said, noticing the weed kick in and imbue my attitude with an oft-absent sense of charity. "This is good shit," I added, by way of compliment.

She smiled back at me, rather noncommittally. But I knew I was dealing from a position of strength and that she wasn't. It was nothing to go and sit at her feet, kneading her calves with hands experienced in such matters. Not much more of a challenge to press my face into the flesh of her bare inner thighs, and to run my hands under the hem of her shorts. When she vaguely protested that she hadn't shaved, I did my best to put her at ease.

"It doesn't matter. What's here is real, and beautiful."

She smiled at me, and it occurred to me that I wasn't entirely running an angle here. To some degree, I meant what I was saying.

"Beautiful," she murmured. I wondered if she'd taken painkillers. If she had, then I wondered if she had some extras.

It's never a risk to put in a Stereolab CD when trying to seduce someone so clearly on the rebound. This is what I did – "you have to hear Ping Pong; it's so good" – and it, coupled with strategically lit candles (ironically, a remnant of my last serious girlfriend who left me with a formidable collection of artsy candle holders as some sort of consolation prize) provided a comely setting for love, exciting and new. Leaving her outside while fetching more beverages, I noticed with considerable alarm that someone might just call me on the phone. Thinking quickly, I unplugged it from the wall. The doorbell was flawed beyond repair, and that was fine as well; the outside world could kiss my ass.

After retrieving the beverages and ensuring that all outside entrances were secure, I returned to Michelle, still lingering on the balcony. From the east, a pleasant breeze had begun to make itself noticeable, bringing with it the husky aroma of coffee from the Maxwell House factory downtown. She had rolled another joint, and we lied down on the shag rug, staring at the stars shining surprisingly clearly in the distance. Physicality took course, and we had sex, though not great sex; she insisted upon being on top, for one thing. As well, she clearly hadn't been with a man for a while, as she pogo-ed rather than concentrated on the slow, careful satisfaction of my needs. But I made sure I stayed hard and came at an appropriate time; this was sex with a pretty blonde 21 year old, after all. An important notch on my all-too-unmarred bedpost. Who cared, really, if she lacked in technique? One could still have an orgasm.

And of course the orgasm happened, and then the drama began in earnest.

I suppose I must have said some things during the prelude to our physical encounter. Michelle had painted a vulgar picture of domestic squalor with Samantha; clearly they weren't getting along. Trying to play up the kindness in my heart, it's not altogether unfeasible that I asked Michelle to stay with me for a while. A few days, perhaps. I'm sure I offered to drive her to her apartment to get some clothes and toiletries. I've said stranger things, really.

Little did I know she would take me up on my offer.

4:30 on a Friday morning. My neighborhood was bathed in pre-dawn quiet, as even the professional indigents had found a dumpster to sleep in or something. The only noise came from Michelle and me as she trashtalked her ex and I feigned listening as we walked toward my car.

"That stupid bitch comes up to my work and accuses my manager of hitting on me. I can fucking handle myself," she said as we got in my compact.

"True," I interjected.

"I'm sick of her. I don't love her the way she loves me and I've tried to tell her that, but she doesn't listen. She's always pawing me, and listening into my phone calls, and she won't leave me alone!"

"Michelle," I said, looking her directly in her eyes, working the sensitive voice for all it was worth. "Listen to me. You had a good run with her. A long relationship. But you need to grow." I stopped the car at a stop sign and ran my index finger along her forearm, as if looking for a vein. "You know?"

I could see that she was buying my voice cracking on the last question. "Yeah," she replied. "I know."

I leaned over to kiss her on her lips, anticipating a lush, heartfelt consolidation of lips and tongue. But there were just lips on her end, as unyielding and stark as breakfast links on a Waffle House plate. We drove on toward her apartment, silent except for when she imparted directions.

She asked me to wait in the car. A few minutes passed, and then I started hearing glass shattering and shrill voices coming from her building. I knew where this was headed. Nasty breakups even involving people who are sane, smart, together, and so forth allow for precious little decorum; breakups between folks who aren't particularly bright are even worse, I've found. All of us have seen Cops or Springer and know how white trash live, but until you hear the phrase "I'll kick your nigger-loving ass" from real people, you're missing a certain knowledge of how these things go down. How restraining orders are planted and then bloom like flowers in Disney landscaping. How people end up in fistfights in Burger King parking lots, and how that sort of thing makes police reports and other repositories of the public record.

I turned on the overhead light and delved into the Paris Review. Same old boring crap poems with ostentatious bullshit words: hydrangea, veranda, eiderdown, and other timid workshop crap. Impulsively, I threw the journal out of the passenger side window. It landed in a puddle.

Just as I was considering the symbolic weight of this action, I heard Michelle rapping on the hatchback glass. "Come help me get some stuff," she urged.

I couldn't refuse; I'd already come this far.

Michelle led me a stairwell with peeling paint on its walls and over some length of indoor/outdoor carpeting redolent of urine and despair. I couldn't imagine living like this, I thought just as I stepped over a cat that could fairly be decided as comatose. Michelle was mouthing off about Samantha again, so it saved me the trouble of making an ass of myself and commenting on the squalor.

We walked into a wide-open door and I took in the contents of the apartment, which looked like it had been raided very recently. CD Jewel cases, empty jars of mayonnaise, and other miscellany were scattered willy-nilly on the floor as if confetti. "Damn," I said because there was little else to say.

"Samantha never cleaned up. Two years we were together and she never cleaned the house once."

"I see."

We made numerous trips to my car, carrying a full-size stereo, large box speakers, crates of records, and armfuls of clothes. It was like a hurricane evacuation, or that pivotal scene in a Lifetime movie when the battered wife packs her car and escapes the hell her life had been for however many Nielsen quarter hours. The afterglow of sex had begun to wear off, replaced by a very real exhaustion as I started to realize that I had created quite a mess for myself. Taking a girl from a disaster-zone tenement rat trap and importing her into my apartment with its Pottery Barn this and that was a dubious proposition at best. Yet I did it, and while we were eating Hardee's breakfast biscuits on the way back to my apartment, I even told her I was happy she was there.

Days passed and we settled into a routine: psychotropic drugs when we could afford them, weed and alcohol even when we couldn't afford them. Michelle, an adept sneak-thief, had no quarrel with liberating bills from her till at work or wallets from the back pockets of overstuffed yuppies at nearby fashionable bars. I had no qualms either; I damned sure wasn't paying her keep.

For about two weeks, sharing living space with her was acceptable. Then the drugs got old, the money ran out, and conflicts arose.

My first real fight with Michelle began innocently enough. She'd cut out of work early and we'd decided to do some shopping in chain stores: she wanted a tech vest from Old Navy and I wanted to do a cost-benefit analysis of CD Burners at Circuit City. Additionally, she wanted to go to Barnes and Noble to get a tattoo magazine or some such. An evening of inoffensive entertainment that no one could reasonably object to.

But I'm not a reasonable person.

Any number of things could've set me off. Perhaps it was the utter incompetence of the clerk at the bookstore when I asked about a certain journal. Maybe it was the disagreeable iciness of my Starbuck's Frappucino. Or it could've been having to explain to Michelle who Neil LaBute was and why we should rent Your Friends and Neighbors instead of some blockbuster piece of crap with an Aerosmith or Creed theme song.

In any case, I became intemperate on the last leg of our foray into the outside world, the drive from the video store to my apartment. "I'm so sick of this bullshit town," I declared. "Nobody here has a clue about anything – stupid, stupid people." I went on in this manner for some time.

"Are you talking about me?" A reasonable question to be sure, and in fact an accurate hunch from lovely Michelle. But I couldn't let her know that.

"No, not you." I exhaled demonstratively. "I'm just stressed out. You know?" I put my arm around her and tried to pull her close to me, to make her body relent its tension; no dice. There was no give, and I retracted my proffered limb.

When we finally got back to my place, she immediately grabbed her address book and took it and the cordless phone into the bathroom. A bad sign, made worse when she emerged a few minutes later. "I'm going out."

"That's good," I lied. "You should go out; we aren't glued together."

She smiled nervously. "Do you mean that?"

"Of course I do. If I don't give you space when you need space, why would you ever come home?" I'd heard people speak this pabulum, but never thought I could successfully pull it off.

She came over to where I sat on the couch and kissed me on the cheek. "I'll be home in a couple hours – not too late."

"I'll save the movie for you; it's really good."

Hours piled onto each other, as it happened, and still no Michelle. I lied on my couch for hours watching a Facts of Life marathon and wondering how it was that the producers thought it a good idea to inflict Geri Jewell on the world. I checked the phone for a dial tone on a couple of occasions. At around 3:30, I finally drifted to sleep.

She returned home at 8:00, signaling her arrival with a sharp knock on the door. "I need a key so I don't have to wake you when I get home," she declaimed.

A key, I thought. A key for a girl who spends every day ripping off her employees and every night submerged in a substance-fueled haze. I held my thoughts. "I'll try to get one made today. I'm just reluctant, still. Things are new, you know?"

We shared breakfast and then she went off to a job. And I pulled some clothes on and visited a familiar location.

As if trying to make a far-flung connection at an airport, I walked briskly over the urine-vitiated indoor/outdoor blend and knocked on Samantha's door with vigor. To my surprise, she opened up.

"Hey . . . what are you doing here?" She asked this while squinting, even though the hallway was darker than her apartment.

"I just wanted to come by, see you. See how you were doing." I looked at the sags and folds of her body, a deterioration well beyond her years; she looked 35 but in reality was much younger, and came off rather blowsy and floozy-like. I could see Bill Clinton sleeping with her.

"Oh, God – I'm half naked." And she was – she wore only a black bra and a sheer white skirt that was twisted around her torso, exposing her underwear on the seam. "Come in, won't you?"

She went into the bathroom to make herself somewhat more presentable, all the while maligning Michelle for my benefit. When brushing her hair, she rattled on about how Michelle kissed like she was trying to ram her tongue down her throat. While donning a different outfit, she managed to work in a reference to Michelle jacking her ex-boyfriend's jungle record collection. And so forth; she was to breakup dish what Ezra Pound was to poetry, perhaps without the idiosyncratic political leanings.

She emerged from the bathroom without words, but with tears running down her face. I pulled her in to my arms to comfort her, feeling her warmth and her adiposal softness through her hotpants and halter top.

And then I had a brainstorm. How many guys get to pull something like this off? So what if it wasn't ideal. Tinker to Evers to Chance, as it were. I had to at least give it a shot.

I asked her if she wanted to get something to eat and she accepted. She was one of those three pack a day, two book a year girls; the kind that started smoking cigarettes at 15 to look cool and older, the kind especially susceptible to polysyllabic bullshit over breakfast at an indie diner. I found myself encouraging her to write a novel, for example, after she told me that she should write one about all the "crazy shit" she'd been through. I also found myself picking her legs up and settling them in my lap, where I started going to work on her calves; though she looked at me with eyebrows raised, she allowed me to go through my paces. Eventually, though she continued to slam Michelle for my benefit as well as that of people at surrounding tables, she seemed to relax. To give into pleasure.

It wasn't really that much of a stretch, then, to entice Samantha to come to my apartment. "We could smoke out, and just get to know each other," I said. "I think you're a really good person." She agreed with but a shadow of reluctance.

Samantha's good vibe was fleeting as soon as we went through my front door. Michelle's belongings were scattered throughout my pad; her bicycle, turntables and mixer, and boxes of clothes were merely notable among the assembled. "The fucking bitch," she sighed. "Can I ask you something?"

I felt her hand clasp around mine, imbued with real urgency that could pass as desire in certain contexts. I was confused and pleasantly surprised; after all, this was a girl that three times in our limited acquaintance had told me that she could have any guy she wanted, but guys just didn't do anything for her.

"Shoot, baby." The baby a trial balloon; she didn't shoot it down.

"You two . . . don't sleep together, do you?"

I pulled a frown. "Of course not. I understand that you two are working things out." I stared Samantha dead on. "We're just friends. She's a lesbian, remember?"

Samantha exhaled. "Yeah, but I know how she is. She fucks anything that moves."

I stood up and went in the kitchen to get Samantha and I a couple of beers. "Well, a lot of us fuck a lot of things a lot of times."

"Yeah," she said, getting up from the couch. "This is true. I have to take a piss."

Samantha closed the bathroom door behind her. I reached into the kitchen cabinet and got a bottle of pills out that I saved for certain occasions. After liberating the tablet from its container, I used a handy garlic press to beat the pill into powder. From there it was no trouble whatsoever to drop the grains into her longneck.

The bathroom sink had been running for some time. After it finally had been turned off, I had been on the sofa for a minute or two, waiting for events to progress. "I got you a beer – let me get that weed out of the gettin' place, all right?" She nodded; her blotchy, dispirited face might have been quite affecting, if I hadn't been in game mode. But I was a baller. A shotcaller.

She sipped her beer and monopolized the pipe, and I came to realize I knew this type too well: the sort of girl that drinks until oblivious and who smokes until there's nothing left. She buried her face in her hands, as if she were a grief-stricken metal god in a video; I pulled her close toward me, and felt her weight collapse into my own form.

She didn't protest when I stretched her out on the sofa. She didn't protest when I lifted her legs so that I could sit underneath them. She didn't protest when I parted her legs with my hand like a jungle explorer clearing out brush.

As my fingers glided toward her center, she purred, "What are you doing? Why don't you . . ."

I whispered back to her, as huskily as possible. "Why don't I what?" Her eyes were closed. Her breathing had lost the jaggedness of arousal and had given way to the pacific static of unconsciousness. Words were beyond her. And I was beyond taking requests. The afternoon's entertainment had begun.

6-4-3.

“MackDaddy:DaddyMack; an identity equation”

A given like a-squared
            plus b-squared
          equals c-squared
that we would hookup
if and only if we were
under the influence
of sundry domestic brews
and a shared affinity
for four-on-the-floor
ec
  stacy

A given like a circumference formula
that you’d pounce on me
like a Bombay on catnip
grind on me
              your eyes closed
as if grating my pelvis
      granting my fondest wish
I concentrated on staying hard
even though
                you are who you are
and I was pulling the niftiest
          of straight white male tricks: hookup after
                                                          hookup after
                                                                   hookup
                                                with chicks who invariably
                                                looked like Chloe Sevigny

at least, that’s how I framed it
over long-distance wires
engendering mimetic crises
saying I fucked it and you did not.

I called fair catch
the possession arrow is pointing
                    pointing
          pointing
toward my groin.
The mack daddy and the dad
dy mack
          That KrissKrossian rap
          so elegant, yet so ambivalent.
But all of this
is just aside and hubris.

Fucking a girl you barely know
is like
          fucking a poster on the wall
a childhood jackoff flight
          of fancy
an ass-out bent over
          bimbo in cutoffs
with her thumb jerking
backwards, toward ME
          (mack daddy: daddy mack; it is an identity equation, mother
fuck
          er)
Asking, are you going to go my way?

We dream of the other.
The straight life, the straight line, the straight girl
is just constraint, restraint, sleight of hand
          flat out lie
We want that which does not
     want us,
that which does not want
     what we want
for our reasons, stacked
so neatly like firewood

in a Merrie Melodies backyard.

We dream of taking a shell,
implanting a new harddrive,
new tits, new ass,
and an attitude that says completely yes:
Begat, Begat, Begat.
          Patrilineal
Jefferson and his slaves
Shawn Kemp and his babymama's spawn.
If giving a fuck is right, I'd rather be wrong.

Like a watch, I'm sprung
free
of repentance.
Bling! Bling!
I just don't give a fuck.
THIS is why I rushed this hookup
          like every other hookup
Preying on weakness and vice
          piercing inhibitions
Big pimpin... Big, pimpin...
Big pimp seeks emotional gimp
New Jack hustla seeks solace.
The Mack Daddy seeks
          Daddy seeks
something like a new

beginning
or an acceptable end

"Still Life in Bayonne"

My dad wasn't much
for parallel parking at 55;
Caddy slotted in ass-out
after a 14 hour drive. Frowns
and scowls from local punks
in dyspeptic sedans, blasting
bass music in treble.

Informer… I'll lick your boom boom
down.
Why worry?

Up the stairs, the hallway
stillness shattered by our jackboot
stomps. Dad's gray face
turned back to me, a lump of salt.
Sorry for showing you death unpolished.
Sorry perhaps for not showing you sooner.
As if.

A faintly beating
Alpine heart. Bobby Brown. *Ain't*
nobody humping around….

Images, jumpcut beyond
cohesion. Pancreatic blots
on kitchen linoleum; eviscerated Lady
Borden cartons blooming
from the pregnant plastic
trash can; Swing the Mood
on the kitchen AM. A cold,

cold house heated only
by a space
heater.
I looked down,
all purple Crosscolours,
all green Doc Martens,
thinking myself exempt
from growing up with a Baltic
heart. From setting the old adrift,
from boxing ancestors for attic
storage.

He's a coldhearted snake.
Look into his eyes.
Whoa, ho. He's been telling lies.
2AM, outside the guestroom window;
Paula Abdul as urban oracle,
scoring two corpulent wops'
doomed courtship in a Primered Nova.
Tell me, Helen. Whatever happened
to Sinatra?

Tell me, Helen.
You cry to no one at night.
Who will feed me?
Who will love me?
Who is left who won't rob me?
Who is left?
Me me me me me me me.
Neglected elderly like birds
chirping in forlorn
cages in empty
homes that aren't
homes at all, that yearn
with the sadness:
generations quashed;
fathers stifling daughters
mothers cuckolding sons.

You knew this well, Helen,
how lineages splintered like branches
broken like broken glass.

Your live at home son,
a dead Olsewski at 60,
pastured driver of Bayonne's
unassuming buses.
Single-leg amputee;
cholesterol victim,
too attuned to the pleasures
of Parkay and Merita,
the pleasures of polka
discs in a joke ethnic tongue.

You two, conjoined.
Yearning for happy endings
Never thinking that mothers, sons
could live and die and burn and burnout
from lust
in raggedy-assed rowhouses.
That mothers could outlast sons.
That none of this would be his.
That no matter how ill
you got or how loud
you turned Wheel Of Fortune up
the spic nurse would still
ransack the silver
that the bills would still
fall through the front door sliver.
That there would be no peace!
That the Pope and the proxy priest
would be dead
set on you not relinquishing
this gift of life!
How lucky you have been!
How many good years.
Never mind the wheezing,

the uncertain, water-logged breaths.
Consider always God's
plan, Widow Olsewski.
Never mind
that you will never stand.
Helen.

Catholic long past incontinence.
Retaining prayers, litany, Latin
chants even after viscera
and faith slumped to mush.
Hail Mary, the neighborhood has gone to shit and
yes, I've forsaken the spirit.
I try to live by the letter
even as waste
seeps in my regions nether.

Hail Mary.
Full of Grace,
please fill me.
Blessed are those bowed
in body and spirit
Blessed are those who
fail as force of habit.
Blessed are we blessed.

“Black Celebration”

Depeche Mode all during my post
Sophomore geometry summer school session;
 me lusting after a goth chick, all angles
and lines. Black Celebration.
Every post-Euclidean afternoon found
 me skulking back to my parents’ tract
home, solemn as a supplicant,
immersed in rituals of self- abasement.
Creak creak go the springs; always
in dreams, I was gaunt, to the lures
of fried food resistant.
So it goes. So it never went.

The loss I felt, always total,
even as I knew not what was lost.
As a Junior, I went industrial, to the Fronts:
Line Assembly. 242, even as cocks
revolted and all pop klinged and klanged,
I still blasted Music For The Masses;
industrial was just a complement.
Yet my bedroom posters corresponded:
the junction of junkyard
chic and concentration camp.
Never was a body unmangled,
an image free of distortion,
a soul lifted from anguish.
I borrowed eyeshadow every weekend,
fell in with a skinny-ass Flip
whose specialties were tarot and blowjobs.

Never wear fishnets to Catholic school.
Never peruse Ginsburg in bio classes led
by baseball coaches. Don’t blast the sound

of Wax Trax from your ride
unless you want a can of whoopass
courtesy of the Aryan Brotherhood of Christian Lettermen.
That's how it all came to pass. I got into astrology.
My future, present, past: occluded, cloudy.
Strange highs and strange lows....

Senior year: I worked the mad face,
psychopathic glint in my eyes,
cursing as if blessed with Tourette's.
I had mastered the trick.
One year in every ten I manage
to drop the dummy crutches,
frame performance art as damage.
To invert succor into curse words,
to let discord begin with me,
to start a modest fire,
to douse it with gasoline,
to borrow a mother's infant
and drop it in for kindling.

Reach out. Touch faith.
The bedsprings klanged
 and klinged in harmony.
At times there were worlds
beyond my room and my head.

“Trucker seeks. . .”

The loneliness of the open road.
How the gravel seems to drone on,
hopeless, wailing, an abandoned mother
liberated only from respite.
Hitchhikers; handlebar mustaches,
muscle shirts, faded-out blue jeans
templates of despair, but still of desire.

Warnings from the dispatcher.
Never, ever stop.
For no reason can you ever stop.

Air brakes themselves with a wistful tristesse,
but it’s too late to phone your mother.
10 PM, well past her threshold.
She’s got the cancer down in Birmingham.

Truckstop shower stalls so inviting.
Nakedness, purity, cleanliness, life.
A boon companion makes his way in.
Hale and hearty, expansive.

Is there room enough for two?
His calloused hands caress so gently,
and it’s so much like the boys’ ranch
or that 8th grade slumber party
where you figured out what Careless Whisper
might’ve meant.

Time can never mend.
But well-placed lips can
shield your throbbing cock
and it’s all just like tenth grade

and it's all just like twelfth grade
and it's all just like the
ads
the discreet I saw yous,
the nervous sidelong glances
the backhanded brushes against
denim-clad phalluses.
Guilty feet have got no rhythm!
But shame-fueled lips suck the hardest,
even as a public shower's torrent
slows to a trickle.

Tonight the music sings so loud.

There can be no expiation.
Only momentary release.
Your destination; many hours away.
Mostly backroads
Your last trophy girlfriend,
backwoods cheerleader.
Knocked up, dealt with.
Dropped off
after the procedure.
You never called. She wrote.
You never answered.
Trucker seeks trucker.
Clandestine hot M on M action.
Trucker seeks midnight fucker.

“Occupant Restraints”

The summer I threw you over
Like chum from a fishing boat
was when I chose
          bodies over souls

I took in girls like I
          was running some sort
of home for the wayward,
confused,
          broken.

Every girl had different rules:
some had to leave when I said
they had to go;
some never got keys
some had busted lips and bruised spirits,
          and if you know me
you know I wasn’t into healing
love with me was like scarlet leaves on dying trees
love is like a heatwave with no respite
          and I make that double
for chicks under my sheets in my bed.

Occupant restraints.
They all had them.
No phone calls, for one.
If they wanted to
make a call, they could walk down
          to the corner
like any other

          occupants:
The bottle-blonde, feigned innocence

a refugee from Sawgrass parents,
whose eyes shimmered
as if in refraction of penetration;
the dark-skinned college gal
she had a boyfriend, but didn't
know how or why
to break his heart so decisively
that he would never forget her name.
And others, always others.

I took them home.
I broke them in.
Days passed, sometimes weeks.
I threw them out.
The cycle would begin again
as more leaves fell from more trees
and the air grew still colder.

“Chelsea”

Chelsea and I talk
As if I lacked a cock
As if I bloomed estrogenic
As if I were her rock.
I know her, though we’ve never
Fucked; chastity belts safely locked
I know
Chelsea

Between us, a chainlink fence;
Sturdy fences; predictable friends.
A water pipe, cheap red wine,
Incense platonic kisses
With lips, never with tongues.
She’s a loose slot, pays off for all
But me.
For her lock, I lack a key,
But luck is just luck.

Chelsea
Once fucked Ice-T
As Body Count’s groupie.
Worked striptease
At a gentleman’s tiddy bar.
Never loved anyone
but Chelsea.

“Cats that meow”.

What is ours anymore?
A house full of steel and wicker,
of chirpy pastels
that belie our singular curse.
Cats that piss
on rugs and chairs
because there is no love,
the tile too stained,
the coffee too bitter.
The breach betwixt our hearts.

Outside, behind us, the landlord’s plot:
A holy-roller, a wife,
a parcel of brats. Curs gnash
their teeth and growl
as I try to get it up.
This isn’t working.

Let’s assume you were right, completely,
even though this poem is mine alone.
You’d still walk out that door,
rattling keys as I wailed. You’d strip
the bed of pillows and sheets
jack the pot from my dresser drawers,
speed off in your Honda, cellphoning,
getting blunted and blasting Fiona.
Limp.

The cats sit behind a bolted front door,
meowing, one note, tuneless repetition.
Before the thing itself knowing what is broken.

“Flying creatures returned to earth”

He’s ashed on his pants again,
so he brushes off and reaches for his
creased, twice-read month-old
Harper’s
he bought during a Charlotte layover.
7 AM.
The lounges are still dead.
Newark at ten, maybe time then
before the banquet for one,
for a couple.

The miles pile up on his account:
his daughter, she travels, with boyfriends.
She accepts them, but this habitué of terminals,
he’s locked out of her graduation.
This devotee of Seven Habits and American Express,
“due to limited seating arrangements…
regretfully.”

Sets of legs, pleated skirts, silk-blend slacks:
girls with carryons as big as their torsos.
Boarding school girls, matched sets.
Broker’s girls whisked away to learn
the value of ethics; Scarsdale, Bethesda
girls who know already
the value of cosmetics; of preparation.
“Just like a woman” on Muzak.
A few of the chests already have begun to bloom.

His instinct’s to leer, but he hitches his waistband. Instead.
They say uncooked rice, if you eat it, you lose weight.

Groups of two or three
seated seraphim
chatting nervously
they do not notice him sharing
the afterbirth of winter break.

"Gemini"

Groups of two or three
seated seraphim
chatting nervously
they do not notice him sharing
the afterbirth of winter break

Gemini on the cusp
of slitting your throat
and bleeding you kosher.
Nothing personal; things
go better with mindfucks,
with the cold, pure
knowledge
that everything is less than it seems.

Friendships die like K-Mart
goldfish. I was
a Navy Brat, early I learned to act,
to seek the main stage sacrosanct.

Let me see that

Thong. Vulnerability
behind that thong,
beneath the callow tan.
This mic is on, I'm on
the cusp
of distraction, consumption,
draining, sucking your bones like marrow,
expelling clean and pure
into our pure and clean
smalltown air.

All girls on the cusp
of being empty husks.
We'll never be more than friends.

“Michael”

I knew Michael back in the day –
he was what you’d call normal, never
hunching over coke bottles
melting fire ants into the sidewalk
like my other so-called boon companions.
Michael just read a lot of sports magazines,
chewed gum when he got stressed out.

I looked up to Michael when
he had the Volkswagen bug with the vintage
8 Track setup.
We’d drive around the treelined industrial parks of
Baymeadows
listening to Astral Weeks, siphoning
gas from dormant late model sedans.
Sometimes one of my three week girlfriends would be there,
crammed in the back, smelling of
porcine sweat.
I always dated fat chicks good for piling clothes on.

Sometimes we went back to my mom’s apartment,
had death matches in Atari
Real Sports Football for the 2600
We thought we were so fucking groovy and camp,
listening to the full length Lipps Incorporated
Funkytown,
waiting for Melissa to hitch a ride from Arlington
with some alcoholic itinerant gardener.
Those were good times then, worthy
of a Hilfiger ad campaign.

I don’t want to wait for our lives to be over.

Michael retailed and stayed still,
Miss Havisham without the vintage dress.
Who's going to love you if you aren't for sale?
Who's going to buy you at seven an hour
when five ought five does just as well before
taxes, he asked.
Michael sold dishes in Mervyn's housewares section.
He traded in the bug for a Datsun or something,
and played Dave Matthews on cassette.

Let's talk about sex.
Humping random broads under stages
of sulky discotechques,
seeing no irony in lambadaing
a Baptist to Rage Against The Machine.
Fistfucking a pregnant black girl
in a pre-Jaguars eastside dump,
keeping an ear cocked for your car
alarm,
redneck coffee perking in the
background.
Michael wasn't about that.

Often you'd see Michael
at KMart,
his eyes lingering on boat children
on the motorized carousel.
His head would bob slightly
to the festive, yet tinny music.
When things got slow he'd steal change
from young entrepreneurs selling World's
Finest chocolate for charity.
He would then collect a wayward
girl from the toy section,
treat her to an Icee,
and watch her as she rotated
to her heart's content.

His mother refused to comment
when I voiced concerns about
him becoming a YMCA counselor.
It was nearing summer 1995.

Michael had begun gaining weight
his frame couldn't quite handle.
He had the belly of a much older man,
a smorgasbord warrior,
well-schooled in the blue collar trades.
His vestigial breasts rose like anthills
underneath the fibers of his shirts. Triple X.
Yet he still rebuffed Erica, who fucked all her friends
(but all of this is his word).

The YMCA refused him,
but AOL took him on.
His mother had started sleeping with her
secretary. There was a scandal.
There were Melissa Etheridge cds.

I knew Michael before he was famous,
and I can't say I loved him,
but I probably won't testify all the same.

“looking for Bob”

We met through Folio,
we had
dinner together
at Red Lobster. We went
to your place.
I remember your books, the pool surrounded
by a high fence. I loved
your silver hair.

I was young once, you know.

You specialized in the new American classics,
Grisham and King, and for humor,
Dave Barry.
The pictures on the mantle, your hair
wasn’t silver there.
First full and jet black,
then graying with a combover.
But everyone gets old.

And you couldn’t keep a woman
for very long. In every frame,
there was a new armpiece,
younger than you every time.
I wondered would my luck hold out.
You plied me with vermouth and recycled lines.

Red Lobster was a blind date, don’t think
I didn’t sense
your keen disappointment.
You eyed the hostess and I couldn’t blame you.
I saw you look with pity
at my gnarled hands.

I had a husband once, though, who never pitied.
He tumbled down icy steps before he could retire.
He left me provided for, comfortably enough.

You talked of timeshares in Jekyll Island.
You were looking for that special someone.

The evening was chill and swimming
was out of the question.
I leaned closer to you
as we skirted the inside
of your tactful wooden fence.
Dogs in surrounding yards
growled and banged against the boards.
You patted me on the back,
I felt terminal.

I loved your silver hair.
You had crab legs
at Red Lobster.
You insisted on paying my way.
All I had was salad.

Church-lady gossip never fails to undermine.
My confidants turned on me,
selling me out, trading
dish for uncovered dish.
I was a pathetic wretch, a voyeur
1.99 a minute, 18 and over.
(And so soon after Abner's
demise).

You told me you'd meet me.
You'd come with me to church.
You cancelled, I understood.

We had dinner at Red Lobster.
I loved your hair, so silver.

“I think of your name”

Not as that of stale
from the box cracker trash,
nor as unstressed/stressed/unstressed
twice, inexorably
ultimately stressed,
nor as that of
a chick too scantily dressed
arms folded over chest,
mélanged seduction and regret.
No, it’s none of that.
Rather, your name, the rhyme,
mere predictor.
Nothing more, nothing less.
Rhyme, whether slant or direct.
or fictive or authentic
never pans out.

With your name, it was no surprise;
Despair and release
as simple and as bleak
as a frat boy pissing
on a snowbank
at 2AM, bereft, adrift,
the ugly one – cleaved from friends
with better clothes and choices
in girls. There could never be surprise
for you or for him, souls
entwined; the college boy
and the callow girl.

Dashboard LED clock; no tick-tock,
just digits clipping past five
as your harpy voice hearkens back

to dismal fights about bank
or its tragic lack;
all the bills and how the money
went – beers and pills,
reefer as reliever sometimes,
but apparently not often enough.

The radio pimps tattoos and all things
attainable, even as traffic throngs
ensconce us on the Fuller-Warren,
as four lanes merge onto a thong,
as you reduce our history
to the prick of a pin;
footnoted, fast food, a whim.
Not like him, Bubba Jim
or whatever his hicktown
character stock
salt of the earth
prick of the week name might be,
the boy with whom you hope to breed
when money isn't so tight.
We bleed through traffic clots
as you say you love him;
he's what a man should be,
not effete, indecisive, me.
I scope out the triangle of
the bottom of the bikini
I scored for you; I owned
that once. Worked it like an abacus,
all fingers, toes, thumbs.
Ancient Chinese secret, huh?
[You caution me, again;
don't be sarcastic, even in poems.
Be a nice person;
I'd sooner shed melanin]

I think of your name,
a candle flicker in my soul

the 6th circle of my hell,
a nudge for me to maim
myself and call
it art. Somewhere,
sometime, someone will
hug you goodbye and it'll
just be a hug.
Everything will be linear,
no one forced to configure
your name into a sign
to work kitchensink
tragedy into ersatz art.
And then you and he can fall
in love sensibly over car payment books,
over acceptable looks over acceptable meals.

"Last Rites for a first kiss."

Landlocked, diminished by distance from the ocean
our entwined bodies desiccated
by all that is Gainesville.
Lately your underwear's always on my floor.
Balls of lingerie, only erotic
when a mother's or a nun's
:never erotic when simply a coed's.

Our first kiss. Air of Gonesh,
sounds of Jane's Addiction.
Goosebumps on your arms when I touched you.
I thought I was special, but you
moved like a pro.
Biting my lip when we kissed.
Sucking my nipple for context.
Jane says, I'm done with Sergio.

And would we be next week?
Would we be covered dish?
Would we arm-in-arm our way down 13th?
Jane says, I'm going away to Spain.

I dumped both my home girls.
You cut ties with home.
Our first was the best lay.
I'd never made a girl come.

I want them if they want me.
I only know they want me.

You're easiest fled when zonked on K.
This final time, I pruned away your limbs.

Finally, inexorably, back home.
Back to the ocean, back to
Fletcher girls, who sucked me off
for cigarettes; don't ask.
They who let me crash
who gave me cash
boosted from parental billfolds.

Always, back to hometown daughters.
They who understood how water was light,
and why they always had to pay my way.

“No room service, just snacks and shit”

The call to ball
heeded as by Pavlov’s
rope-a-dope pups:

Two tricks in a deluxe
suite ecstatic
exempt from commitment
in self-abasement, complicit.

mouths down, cracks up

on pills, strung out

wear them out
                              flip them up
send them home,

no doubt, separate cabs; no tips, no smile.

“Paid in full”

Sturdy as subdivision homes,
bred for the service industry
racket
with Sex Ed and IALAC and
True Love Waits,
paychecks blown on Pumas
we wear when we stagger
to the temp agency
to pick up paychecks.

You can trust us
like lunchroom milk.
Our torsos sag from too much Denny’s,
too much 2Am. Our fumbling
hands aren’t speaking of shy reserve;
oh, no. We take all we can get.
And you seem shocked

because we’ll piss in any jar
for any corporation
for any no-benefit, nothing
happening wage. But
where would we have learned pride?
From Dan and Donna Hicken
Or a Times-Union column?
And you seem shocked

because we turned out doughy
on one side,
charred to a crisp on the other.
White kids fuck and run now,
big surprise. White kids
got no pride, all pierced navels

overwrought bass bins,
babymamas and babydaddys,
the detritus of a tin-shack culture
founded on obvious irony and sight gags.
There's something about Mary.
And where is our faith in mainstream religion?

And everyone I know's knee deep in
Nine Inch Nails and Club H20
and we can all feel each other up
if we downplay consequence.
Everyone keeps it real, has something to say,
even if the lines are clumsy and the thoughts cliché.
Our pills: signed disclaimers for physical contact,
but even during the ephemeral ecstasy rush
the boys stare daggers into the other boys
because no one wants to come off as soft.

But we persevere, as we do,
sturdy as tract homes, saying
Thank you, welcome, drive through
in our blue polyester vests.

“The Score”

I’m Back from Columbia,
the kid’s been aborted by
a trusted family friend;
I’m at loose ends: sullen,
pout-faced, crossword-focused
yet cross-purposed.
So loose are all my ends.

And if I fuck up again
I’m for sure out on my ass.
If you think Dad’s kidding
when he says get a job,
or else Kent Campus
you’ve got another think coming.
No time to fuck around, he grunts.
Pinned to a closet door
by concrete forearms my eyes
roll back; I lose control
of my mouth. The scene fades
to black.

Friends are distant these days:
church groups, threesomes
in abandoned cars, affairs
unmarked by despair,
where everyone’s nice and chill
and everything free of consequence.
Friends
are very busy
and the boys who used to see me
see other girls
now, girls
whose smile doesn’t splinter

under the weight of severest doubt.

7AM, Sunday.
Dad drops the want ads
on my bare, bare chest.
Check these out Missy,
or I'll take your car and
you're out on your ass.
And where and how to go?
I never know.

Mom knew the score,
though she fucked me up
before she left; took
one look at my breasts,
sucked in her breath,
and said
these newborn blooms
will be your death –
and none too soon.
She screws a sailor up in Norfolk; drunk,
she left a message about
the sweetness of his cock.
Says he makes her young.
Before, she was so old.

March is frozen food month.
Lincoln freed the slaves.
Alanis speaks to me.
I feel the void inside.
It would've been a few months.
I can't keep anything straight.
Publix is hiring baggers.
Publix is hiring slaves.
No one really knows for sure.

"Country Grammar"

Wendy's triple, oozing
with grace mayo grease;
Showtime movies, rated R, (Risky
Business, 1981); sleepovers,
tents of sheets ballasted by bricks
atop the dormant gas heater
in the hall; Mom's common law
Mark punting the coffeetable,
flashbacked to Mekong,
vexed by paychecks anorexic.
Big Deluxe

Hardee's,
loaded sans lettuce, still they taste
like plastic. Starsearch blared
the house throughout on Sunday nights,
a complement to

Shirts and jeans too hillbilly, too tight.
No girl sends Valentines to
double-wide boys in Toughskins, boys
with Dusty Rhodes tits and lisps.
Birthday bashes grim, sparsely attended,
perfunctory as silk Roses on crypts,
marked by odd lacerations
from sundry backyard dangers.

Little Caesar's pizzas in
boogie-board boxes; crabbing
and shrimping Friday nights, crackling
Reds games on the AM band,
a timezone distant. Playing
catch solo in the sandy

front yard, throwing footballs
from self to self, dreaming of
driving, like Mark, a truck.

Cracking the code in Galaga,
4 hours play on a quarter,
Curtis and I jacking
half-drank RCs unattended
at the laundry to sugar
up before smallfry football.
Once, I stomped a prone boy's arm when playing noseguard,
smiling through my mouthpiece. No regrets.

Chicken McNuggets.
9 in a box.
Sweet and sour
sauce.

Then came a hit and run,
an Omni took my 3 speed on;
the Omni won. Comatose
four days, my skull's crown spongy, inviting
like a pin-up's gash.

At home, recovery was intended to pass.
Mark flattened me
in the backyard, grinding
his cock in my face, amidst
overgrown weeds and a kibbutzing Spitz.
He knew desire better than I, and I closed my eyes and hoped for
closure.
Soon poverty would end. Soon the present would become anecdote.
But for then his eyes were glazed with the most recognizable of
wants.
KFC, Original Recipe.
Mashed Potatoes, Gravy
Corn
on the cob.

“Summertime Rolls”

How many nights
did you spend:
trolling the midnight streets
grimfaced, cellphoning
for the MDMA fix?
Your Saturn brimming
with people you could barely stand:
the guy behind you who
used to fuck your girlfriend;
the others, likewise,
you couldn’t recommend.
How many
nights spent?
Nightclubs vitiated by grime,
where the low-end bass fizzled
into static, clinging
to all your friends, so-called.
You tried to front
like you meant the frenzied
swinging of limbs,
like the collapse to be blown up wasn’t somehow
affected.
After parties; well, at least they were closure.
A Callahan doublewide, an anonymous
suck off by a paunchy girl
who reeked of vitiated
feet and Vaporub.
The hearkening of the disco
call rings so distant.
You push her off your flagging cock,
stagger into the lavatory
wonder when last it was cleaned.

Around the drains, the black rings;
the mildewed scowl of her toilet bowl.
All you can conjure is loss.

"Modern Dancers"

I watch my girlfriend dance
with another chick,
limb on limb like icing on cake
                        blanket on sheet
            white on nit
    misconception on Heaven
    misery
on the bedridden

Their arms entwine, then their bodies cleave;
then they reunite
                        cheek to cheek
Her eyes are not fixed on me.
I stare at the
                        concrete.
I watch my girlfriend rehearse;
her face pressed betwixt her partner's thighs.
Peaking like   a cat on nip
                        a raver on a pill
                a runner in the fifth mile
                a gambler on a fated streak.
She spits when she blows me,
balks at the hair on my body;
my pelted chest, my back
                       thistly,

                      anathemic.
My face stubbly, not mythic.
I will never be her God.
I am not rhythmic,
not attuned to the nocturnes
        of DeBarge and Corona.

A chubby white guy, mulleted,
at the discotechque
tragic, neglected,
fluid as grease congealed,
not intended
to be consumed.
Their lips press together.
My paunch buckles my belt's border.
This will be the longest summer;
bereft of redress,
flush with regret.

Acknowledgments

I’d like to thank my mother for her unfailing support
and
Rick Moody for providing a model.

A collection of poetry, espousing the real side of life. The gritty front of the modern world, brought into sharp focus through painfully honet intropspection and examination. A powerful debut work.

Title: Guts
Author: Catherine May
Publisher: Diversity Incorporated
ISBN: 0-9704098-2-6
Price: $9.00 (Trade Paperback)
Pages: 96

Order Form

Please send the following books.

DIVERSITY, INC.

Shoot Out the Lights and Other Stories, by Benjamin M. LeRoy
ISBN 0-9704098-0-X, $9, PDCT#001

Distracted and Other Poems, by Sarah Gajkowski
ISBN 0-9704098-1-8, $8, PDCT#002

Guts, by Catherine May
ISBN 0-9704098-2-6, $9, PDCT #003

Unfortunate Incidents 1996-2000, by Anthony Gancarski
ISBN 0-9704098-3-4, $11.95, PDCT#004

PDCT#________ QTY________ Total$________

PDCT#________ QTY________ Total$________

PDCT#________ QTY________ Total$________

*WI residents add applicable sales tax

Send check or money order to: Grand Total$________

Diversity Incorporated
PO Box 8573
Madison, WI 53708

For credit card orders please visit www.diversityincorporated.com